RHONDA R. ROBERSON

FOREWORD
Bishop Charles L. Middleton Sr.

A
FRIEND
For The
JOURNEY

A FRESH PERSPECTIVE
ON GETTING THROUGH THE GRIEVING PROCESS!

In Loving Memory of:
Min. Carmen D. Murray

A Friend for the Journey
ISBN - 13: 978-0692842584
ISBN - 10: 0692842586
Copyright © 2017
By Rhonda R. Roberson
Published by Rhonda R. Roberson
Email: lohigherground@gmail.com
Cover Design: Mogul Focus (www.mogulfocus.com)
Editor: Pastor Ashaki Moseley

CONTENTS

DEDICATION

The Murray Family

This book is dedicated to the entire Murray family. God has blessed my family and I to be honorary members of this family for a very long time. This book has been written most of all to edify, encourage, and comfort Carmen's precious Mother, Shirley Murray, and Carmen's one and only beloved sister, Cynthia. Over the years, I have had the privilege to see (in a close up and personal way) the power of covenant relationships in action, through the Murray family.

Out of all the challenging things I have seen them go through over the years, I have never had to witness something as devastating as what they went through, in the passing of Minister Carmen Murray—to the church triumphant. I can only imagine the depth of their pain, as I reflect on the depth of my own. From my perspective, their ability to continue standing in faith is a witness and testimony to the awesome amazing grace and power of God to help us through the journey of life.

I pray this little book with bring some measure of comfort, laughter, and rejoicing to your hearts as you reflect on your loved one who lived life so well, in the sight of God and mankind. She is now in a far better place, though she will always be missed more than words could ever express in an adequate way. In spite of it all, I can still hear her saying what the Shunamite woman said in 2 Kings 4:26: *"It is well."* Yes, in the midst of this crisis situation, Carmen said to me, *"Ron, it is well with my soul."*

ACKNOWLEDGEMENTS

My Parents

In memory of my parents, Rev. Albert Roberson and Missionary Luana Roberson, who are now gone on to be with the Lord. They would be amazed to see how the Lord is using their youngest child through writing these days. They were the best parents anyone could have asked or hoped for. I love and miss them so much, and I look forward to our blessed reunion one of these days—after, of course, I have served out my purpose in the earth. I could never thank them enough for the investment they made in my life. I am so thankful to God, most of all for the precious memories I have of them. They are now tucked away in my heart, never to be forgotten.

Mt. Zion NCBC

I want to acknowledge Bishop Charles L. Middleton Sr., Co-Pastor Mary E. Middleton, and the entire Mt. Zion New Covenant Baptist Church of Detroit. I honor you for your untiring labor of love in assisting our beloved sister, Carmen, through the toughest journey of her life, as she went from labor to reward as a child of the King! I bless you in Jesus' name, and thank you, once again, on behalf of the Murray Family as well. We will never forget all that has been done to love, support and encourage us through the grieving process, when we all well know that you were grieving deeply yourselves. May God bless you for that unselfish act of faith, confidence, and trust in our awesome God!

Note: Additional acknowledgements are located in the back of this book.

WRITING BOOKS IN COMMUNITY

My pastor, Bishop Charles Middleton, recently mentioned that he wanted me to read a note from a powerful book called *Celebration of Discipline*, written by a man named Richard J. Foster. On his acknowledgments page, he wrote of people he wanted to thank for their contributions to his book.

What he said was so powerful when you think about it! He said, "Books are best written in community."[1] He went on to say, "I am deeply indebted to those whose lives have surrounded mine, and have given substance to the ideas in this book."[2] He then names one of many of them, Dallas Willard and says, "it was through Dallas Willard, that I first saw the meaning and necessity of the Spiritual Disciplines."[3] God placed us as believers in the context of community life together (as the body of Christ); therefore, our God-given assignments are best fulfilled in this context.

I, too, have had a community who contributed to this book, and I have included them in these writings to bring their own personal perspectives of grieving. You will find these additional writings under "Personal Reflections" in the back of this book. I am thankful to God, first for my writing mentor, Bishop Charles L. Middleton Sr., and Pastor Ashaki Moseley, my faithful spiritual daughter and editor. Also, for my family and friends, for their precious keen insights on grieving, and for sharing from the heart the love they had for Carmen Murray, as well!

Reflections by: Sis. Shartrese D. Roberson
Reflections by: Min. Joshua D. Roberson
Reflections by: Dr. Linda Cobb-McClain
Reflections by: Rev. Doris Moseley
Reflections by: Sis. Sherisse Knight

FOREWORD

Bishop Charles L. Middleton Sr.

In this new writing project, my daughter, Minister Rhonda Roberson, has given fresh meaning to the old word "disciple." By definition, a disciple is one who learns to live the life that his or her teacher lives. Well, Rhonda, like her teacher, lives the life of a "wonderful counselor," and that's what this book is all about: bringing "good news" to people who need it, but can't afford it; release for the captives; vision for those who have none; and real liberation for both the oppressed and the oppressor.

What comes through loudly and clearly in these pages is the fact that helping ministries is a relational service through and through. In other words, for people dealing with grief, a broken heart, or some form of oppression, the need is for a friend **"who will sign on for the journey."** What is not needed is a non-Christian, objective, detached "professional" with no feelings or mind in the matter.

In her journey with Carmen, Rhonda made herself vulnerable in a way that others could never understand. She "took up the cross" and vowed to do the loving thing, knowing that pursuing such a course of action could break her own heart—and it did. She took a hit and came through the ordeal with a limp and a book. Please read it!

It's an easy read; but, more importantly, it is grounded in the revelation of scripture and has been proven in the crucible of ordinary experience. I recommend this practical teaching.

Every believer must learn these lessons — not just for their own benefit, but for the untold numbers of people they know who will need some help in getting through what they need to get through.

ABSENT FROM THE BODY
PRESENT WITH THE LORD

―――――――〜―――――――

2 Corinthians 4:17-18; 5:1-2, 7, 8

For our light affliction, which is but for a moment, worketh for us a far more exceeding and eternal weight of glory; while we look not at the things which are seen: for the things which are seen are temporal; but the things which are not seen are eternal.

For we know that if our earthly house of this tabernacle were dissolved, we have a building of God, an house not made with hands, eternal in the heavens. For in this we groan, earnestly desiring to be clothed upon with our house which is from heaven...

For we walk by faith, not by sight. We are confident, I say, and willing rather to be absent from the body, and to be present with the Lord.

―――――――〜―――――――

INTRODUCTION

A Friend for the Journey is a book designed to give you some timely words of exhortation and comfort, as you go through the grieving process in the passing of your loved one. At the same time, I am seeking to broaden your "perspective" of the faithfulness of God, as you journey through this trying time in your life. Having experienced the passing of my dearest friend and covenant sister on earth, I am now seeking to help others to get through the grieving process by the grace of God. I want to begin sharing with you by first setting the stage of how I came to write this book on grieving, in the first place.

One day during the time when my precious friend Carmen was sick, I went over to her house to keep her company, and assist in any way I could. On that particular day, one of her family members showed up to pray with her. She is such an anointed woman of God, and always has a good word in her heart to release from the Lord. She has the gift of exhortation for sure! Whenever she comes into a room she just lights it up with that loving smile, and a warm loving hug too!

When she came through the door and saw me (not knowing I was going to be there that day), she began to speak to me, in a prophetic way, related to Carmen. As best as I can recall right now, I remember her saying to me that I was going to write a book about "this." However, she did not say exactly what the topic was; she just said "this." That's the way she said it. So, in my mind, I was thinking yes, I totally agree! What I thought she meant by saying the word "this" was about walking through this journey with Carmen toward a miraculous recovery.

I thought, from my perspective, that God was going to allow me to record the miraculous healing, He was going to perform in her body. I thought that it would be amazing for so many people to be able to read about what He had done in her life. That sounded like the faithfulness of our God to me!

So, I started to get excited about it, and I sort of tucked these words away in my heart. Just like Mary the mother of Jesus did in Luke 2:19, where it says: *"and Mary kept all these things, and pondered them in her heart."* After that, I started paying even more attention (spiritually and naturally) to the journey we were on together.

I started making mental notes of what I sensed was going on from day to day. I thought about what an honor it would be for God to trust me with this type of assignment—to record such an awesome miraculous event! Then others would be able to read all about it, for generations to come.

However, as time went on, Carmen did not seem to be making the kind of progress I had anticipated in her health, although she did have some encouraging doctor's reports from time to time. Then I was thinking well, I'm just going to continue to stand in faith and believe God. As the situation grew progressively worse (naturally speaking), she ended up passing away from this expression of life. Of course, being as devastated as I felt at the time, I could hardly even remember the word I had received about writing this book.

Later on, after everything had ended and months had gone by, the Lord began to speak to me again about writing this book. I was feeling kind of puzzled at this point and wondering what was going on.

Human reasoning started kicking in right about then. So, in my mind, I was thinking,

"Why is God still talking to me about this book? What's the point? After all, this book was intended to be about a miracle, not about grieving over the passing of a loved one, wasn't it, God? Did I misread the script?"

That's when the Lord reminded me of a scripture Carmen and I would always quote to one another, when things did not seem to be going the way we planned. Sometimes it was when we were working on a project at church together. At other times, it was when we were going through some type of personal crisis in our lives. The scripture we would quote together is in Proverbs 19:21, and it says, *"There are many devices in a man's heart: nevertheless the counsel of the LORD, that shall stand."*

The New Living Translation of this verse says it this way: *"You can make many plans, but the LORD's purpose will prevail."* Well, that just about says it all, doesn't it! Sometimes our best laid plans just don't turn out the way we thought they would. At times like these we must admit that we just don't know it all. Only God knows the end from the beginning! The truth is that our times are in His hands, not ours (Ps. 31:15).

At the time, it seemed so odd to me that I should write this book, because when it came to a book on grieving, I would always tell Carmen she needed to write a book on this topic. I would say this to her because she had been through some really tough grieving situations as well. She seemed to have some real revelation on this topic, from my perspective.

She would agree with me when I would say that to her, but I sensed in my spirit that she didn't think she would be doing that, for some reason unknown to me, although she never verbally said she would not.

I think she was just being sensitive to the fact that even though this may have been her desire, it was possible that she may not get to fulfill it. She was willing to *adjust* and *adapt* to things not always turning out the way we would like them to at times. The bottom line is that she trusted God, and understood that His ways are just higher than ours, as the scriptures say (Isaiah 55:9).

This is a little snapshot of how I came to write this book (by the grace of God), and I am so glad that I did. Even though the topic of this book did not turn out to be about a miraculous healing in this expression of life (as I thought), it is still about a miracle of a life well lived by the grace of God. It is also about a miraculous transition into the awesome life to come, which is far better! Do I still believe in miracles after all of this, someone might be wondering? My answer is absolute, yes!

One way of understanding what a miracle really is would be to define it as a supernatural event. It is when God, in his divinity, supernaturally intervenes in our lives to make known His will in the earth. It may be an individual or corporate manifestation, expressed in the earth realm in various ways.

This type of supernatural event reminds me of a scene in the book of Luke 1:26-38, when God sent an angel (His messenger) to announce to the virgin Mary that she would miraculously conceive in her womb and bring forth a Son, whose name would be called—Jesus.

Then the angel went on to give her a glimpse of what his destiny would be. As Mary continued to converse with the angel, she went on to "receive" that word. She received that word by saying, *"behold the handmaid of the Lord; be it unto me according to thy word."* (vs. 38.) Then, lo and behold, she conceived the Savior of the world—just as the angel had said. Now that's supernatural! Only God can perform miracles. That's what makes it a miracle, because only he can do it.

Actually, one of the most common words that we find being used in the New Testament for the word miracle is the word "sign." We all know that signs are created in order to *point* to something. Just like when you are in an airport. There are signs all over the place pointing you to the way to reach your destination. God uses signs also, called "miracles," that point to himself as a very real and awesome God!

Jesus performed miracles throughout the New Testament. Those miracles that happen all through the bible (in both the Old and New Testament) were not only happening back in those days. They are still happening today all around us, within us, and even through us, as believers in Jesus Christ. Though I can hardly name them all, let me just name a few of them to encourage you. It's a miracle how God sent Jesus to save us from our sins. He delivered us from the power of darkness and then translated us into the Kingdom of His Dear Son (Colossians 1:13-14). Actually, salvation is one of the greatest miracles of all!

It's a miracle how when we die in the Lord, we are absent from the body, and immediately present with the Lord. Our spirit and soul go immediately into His presence. Now that's absolutely awesome isn't it. (2 Corinthians 5:8).

It was a miracle how God kept Carmen "stable" through the journey from this life to the next, by His amazing grace. It was a miracle how she kept the faith, in spite of all the demonic opposition sent against her on her journey to Christlikeness. It was a miracle how many lives she touched on her way to glory, as she sought for God to get the "maximum glory" out of her life.

The impact that she made was certainly confirmed by the outpouring of love shown by the attendees at her funeral, from all walks of life! The church was absolutely packed to capacity. It was absolutely amazing! It's also a miracle how God is getting the rest of us (left here on earth) through this grieving process, from day to day. Restoration is happening in our lives right in the midst of the pain of it all.

Yes, I must say, as the powerful anointed woman of God named Kathryn Kuhlman use to say on her TV broadcast (many years ago), "I Believe in Miracles!" Yes! And I certainly do too! Actually, you are about to embark upon a miracle as you read the pages of this book! Yes, God is still working miracles and He certainly is not through yet! May you be greatly inspired and encouraged as you receive a "broader perspective" on the grieving process, all for the glory of God!

CHAPTER 1

THE TRUE MEANING OF FRIENDSHIP

"Agree with each other, love each other, be deep-spirited friends...Put yourself aside, and help others get ahead... Forget yourselves long enough to lend a helping hand...Think of yourselves the way Christ thought of himself."

Philippians 2:2-3 (MSG)

"A friend loveth at all times..."

Proverbs 17:17

You never know how or when you are going to run into someone in life, who was ordained by God to be a real friend for the journey of life. I had the pleasure and the esteemed honor of meeting someone who fits that description perfectly. It was an ideal fit, just like a hand in a glove—in the person of Carmen D. Murray. She was just coming out of college, and had somehow found her way to a church that I was already a member of at the time.

I realize now that our steps were being ordered to find each other by the Lord, just as it says in the scriptures (Ps. 37:23). Little did I know that deep down inside she was searching for the real purpose of her life spiritually. She was looking for a "model" to pattern after, of what it really means to be a Christian.

The Lord let her find me in the house of the Lord. I was a member in my church home of a small group of women called "Young Christian Women United."

1

After meeting us, Carmen decided to become a member. We were a mission group made up of single women on a mission in more ways than one.

We were young women who had a vision for living the life that pleases God, by the grace of God. We deeply desired to do something meaningful for Him in the midst of our singleness. We wanted to serve out God's purpose in our lives for being single at this time. We would do things like pray, study the Word of God, have food fellowships, and go on visitations to the sick and shut-in of our church together as a ministry team.

The Model Precedes the Message

In Carmen's life, I had become the model she was looking for (which was so amazing to me) of what living the Christian life really looked like. She told me this some years later as our bond of friendship grew. It was not that I was living my life so perfectly that captured her attention, since nobody is perfect. Perhaps what she actually saw was my inner heart's desire to be *committed* to the will of the Lord for my life. It was such a reminder to me that you never know who is watching you, and looking up to you as a model of the true meaning of the Christian life in word and in deed.

Almost immediately we became attached to each other, and began growing together in the things of God. As I look back on it now, I realize that we were growing together in "covenant" love, which is about "abiding" in a relationship, although we really didn't have a clue back in those days what it meant to be in covenant with one another. We ended up learning this biblical truth much later under the leadership of our new Pastors, Bishop Charles L. Middleton Sr. and Co-Pastor Mary E. Middleton.

This all happened after we both became members of another church called Mt. Zion New Covenant Baptist Church.

We came to understand that to be in covenant had to do with a binding relationship that we entered into, not only with God, but with one another in Christ at the time we were saved. As we submitted ourselves to these teachings, we realized that this covenant had "terms" that we must learn to keep by the grace of God.

A few of these terms were to love one another, pray for one another, bear one another's burdens, forgive one another and there are many more "one another's" that are taken from the scriptures. You will find a list of more of these terms in **Appendix B** of this book. You will also see what a "Covenant Community" should look like when everyone (who is in Christ), is functioning according to the terms of the covenant in **Appendix A**.

As the years of our friendship continued, I noticed that Carmen was living out these terms toward me in such profound ways. She became so committed to praying for me. If I had a problem, she was so concerned about it that you would have thought, it was her own personal problem.

She would call me on the phone and encourage me. Then she would give me scriptures that she had taken the time to look up, in order to help me with the situation. We would pray together on the phone, and cry together too. Then before I knew it she would have me laughing by making some type of joke, just to get a smile out of me. She really understood the power of laughter and maintaining a cheerful heart (Prov. 17:22).

She had such a wonderful sense of humor that you couldn't help but laugh. She was always seeking to make me feel better about the situation. One of her favorite sayings was *"this too shall pass."* So she would say to me *"Ron,* (as she use to call me), *this too shall pass."* At other times, she would use her grandmother's old saying, *"It's a mighty long lane that don't change."* Then we would laugh together.

I also remember how she would pick me up all the time, since I didn't have a car. She would come through rain, sleet, and snow. She would make sure that I didn't miss any important events, church related or otherwise. It might have been a birthday party, or just to hang out together at her house. It never mattered how far she had to go out of her way to pick me up or take me home. She always did it with a smile. Every Thanksgiving and Christmas, Carmen and her family would always invite my family over. My daughter, grandson, and I would go over to her house for a fun time of fellowship and a hot delicious meal, too, with our extended family we called—the Murrays. We always felt so at home whenever we were over there.

You see, my mother no longer lived in the city and my father was deceased by this time, and so being together with them meant a whole lot to my family and I. Carmen was always so sensitive to how I felt at different seasons because I didn't have much family in the city, so she would never let me be alone. One time, when I was sick on one of those special family occasions and couldn't come over to her house, she called me on the phone and said, *"I'm on my way over."* Then she would show up with orange juice, apple juice, water and something to eat, to help me get through this time. She would even come over and wash my dishes and mop the floor if needed. Even if it didn't need it, she was still going to do something to try and help out.

4

You see, I was often sick in those days, because I had been diagnosed with two diseases: Sarcoidosis and Erythema Nodosum. This was back in the early 1990's. The symptoms from these diseases would come and go, affecting my lower extremities, sometimes even making it difficult for me to put on my shoes or even to walk. My feet would be so swollen and painful that I would have to keep them stacked up on pillows to help them go down. So, if I was going through one of those episodes, she would do whatever she could to help make it more bearable for me.

This also included going to the market to shop for me, if I happen to be low (from her perspective) on groceries at the time, and then buying it with her own money. Then she would refuse to let me pay her back, even if I had the money. All of this is why I actually gave her the name "covenant" because she always honored the terms of the covenant, on good days, bad days, happy days, and the sad ones too. She understood the nature of true covenant love in such a marvelous way! It's that "unconditional" kind of love, that flows straight from the heart! It's the God-kind of love!

The Tables Turned

At various times in our friendship journey together, all of the love she would show toward me started to make me feel that our friendship might be too one sided. Even though I had done some nice things for her over the years as well, the things she was doing for me seemed to far outweigh mine. Though I knew in my heart that it was not about trying to have a 50/50 relationship, I still wanted to do so much more for her. I was not trying to be in *competition* with her, but rather, I was just "grateful" for all she had done for me over the years. I just wanted to be more of a blessing back to her in any way that I could.

I remember talking to the Lord several times about this dilemma in my mind. In reality, I knew she was more capable of doing some financial things for me because of the type of job she had. However, I still would sometimes feel bad about not being able to do more for her. Then, suddenly, one day the tables turned—dramatically. My precious friend received an overwhelming diagnosis, and things began to spiral downhill physically—as her health began to deteriorate rather rapidly. It was a serious turning point for us all!

This became one of the most painful times of my life, not to mention what her family was about to go through as well. We were about to enter a crisis situation with a rather uncertain end, in this expression of life, although we knew she was secure for the afterlife, without a doubt!

At the same time, this crisis gave me one of the greatest opportunities of my life. It was about to be somewhat of a "bittersweet" moment in time, for sure! In spite of that, the blessing was going to be that I would be able to serve this mighty woman of God (in a greater way), who had laid down her life for my sake; as a covenant sister beloved. It was now my turn to honor the terms of the covenant in a greater way, and it was indeed my pleasure to do so. I sought to wait on her hand and foot as she faced the greatest fight of faith—of her life. Out of all the physical challenges she had experienced in her life, this one proved to be the greatest of them all. I must say that through it all, her faith in God did not fail.

Watching her during this trial reminded me of a place in the scriptures when Jesus said to Peter (when he was in a tight situation), *"I have prayed for you that your faith may not fail"* (Lk. 22:32)." That was Carmen all the way. She hung in there by the grace of God, and

I am a witness (among many others) that her faith did not fail. She was drawing strength from her union with Him on a daily basis (I Cor. 6:17).

She loved God with all her heart, soul, and mind and her neighbor as herself. She fought the good fight of faith, and she won! Now there is laid up for her a crown of righteousness, and a soul winners crown, too. I can still here her saying right in the midst of it all, *"Ron, God is faithful,"* or at other times she would say, *"What a mighty God we serve!"*

What Can We Learn?

Many of the saints (in my local church and other personal friends) also have similar testimonies of how Carmen lived her life, in covenant love. However, I am only sharing my personal perspective and experiences with you at this time.

I trust after reading some of my experiences on the true nature of friendship or what a true friend really is, that you will take time to learn the terms of the covenant for yourself, then begin walking them out in a greater way with your brothers and sisters in Christ. Please never take your friendships for granted, nor the length of time you may be given to honor them. These covenant relationships take both *giving* and *receiving*. We are to edify (i.e. buildup, encourage) one another in the body of Christ (1 Thess. 5:11).

So, I encourage you to love one another and remember, real love is an action word. It's learning to love others, both in word and in deed. It is learning to love them with an "unconditional" love, just like the love God has toward us. Keeping these terms is not just for those who you are closely related to as friends, but all those who are members of the body of Christ.

7

These are the "covenant connections" that God is trusting us to maintain in the earth. Especially with those who are members of "the household of faith," i.e. the local church (Gal. 6:10). Will it cost you something? Absolutely, it's a life laid down. It will cost you everything, but it will be well worth the sacrifice, when you consider the awesome price that Jesus paid that we might live.

It cost Jesus everything, but through the process He gained many sons of righteousness—that's us! What a friend we have in Jesus! Although Carmen was chosen by God as my natural friend for the journey in the earth realm, Jesus was and is the greatest friend of all times! Where did she learn to be the kind of friend she was to me and so many others? She was following the model of the greatest friend of all—our Lord and Savior, Jesus Christ! I encourage you to follow that same pattern too!

CHAPTER 2

CLEARLY A NEW BREED

"Therefore, if any man be in Christ, he is a new creature: old things are passed away; behold, all things are become new."

2 Corinthians 5:17

"Finally, my brethren, be strong in the Lord, and in the power of his might. Put on the whole armour of God, that ye may be able to stand against the wiles of the devil"

Ephesians 6:10-11

My Pastor wrote a little book a while ago called *The Emerging New Breed*. Out of all the books he has written and I have read over the years, I discovered that I had not got around to reading this one yet. Finally, I got a copy and began to read shortly before my precious sister passed away. As I began to read it, I realized that Carmen was clearly a new breed.

What is a new breed? According to the definition that my pastor used in his book, "The New Breed is essentially concerned with the development and expression of the image of God in His authorized representatives."[4]

In other words, the new breed's focus in this life is all about being conformed to the image of Jesus Christ, and representing Him at the highest level in the earth.

One of the foundation scriptures for this revelation is Romans 8:29, which says:

"For whom He did foreknow, He also did predestinate to be conformed to the image of His Son, that He might be the firstborn among many brethren."

You might say that these new breeds are Christians who are in hot pursuit of the fullness of the will of God for their lives. They seek to operate in a different sphere, and at a different level of authority in the earth realm than the average Christian does.

They understand clearly who they are—in Christ—and that there is an "inward work" that must take place in them, so that they can be a full participant in the end-time ministry assignment given them by God. They spend much time in the secret place with God, longing to see the manifestation of His power and glory operating in and through them so that they can be effective in the earth. It is described as "the high calling of God in Christ Jesus" in Philippians 3:12-16. They have answered this "high calling" in Christ no matter what personal cost they may have to pay to reach this lofty goal.

This type of focused mindset is viewed as a lifestyle from the perspective of the new breed. It is designed to be lived out on a daily basis before a fallen world. They are in liberation ministry and will do whatever it takes to set the captives free in word and deed. They understand that the world must have a model that will precede the message of the good news of Jesus Christ, and they are determined to be that model.

They understand that they don't have a lifetime to fulfil this goal. Therefore, they say along with Jesus, "I must be about my Father's business." This is what I saw firsthand in my friend Carmen. She was passionate about being conformed to the image of Christ and serving out her purpose in the earth.

I remember one day, when Carmen and I were talking, that she told me she wanted to grasp the purpose for which Christ had taken hold of her. She told me that this desire of hers was birthed in her, out of a scripture that the apostle Paul wrote in Philippians 3:12. This is where he said,

> **"Not as though I had already attained, either were already perfect; but I follow after, if that I may apprehend, that for which also I am apprehended of Christ."**

To make this a little bit clearer let's see how the New Living Translation states this verse. It says,

> **"I don't mean to say that I have already achieved these things or that I have already reached perfection, but I press on to possess that perfection for which Christ Jesus first possessed me."**

What the apostle Paul is referring to when he says *"I don't mean to say that I have achieved these things,"* is found in the verses just above this scripture (in Phil. 3:12), where he says these powerful words in verses 10-11 (NLT):

> **"I want to know Christ and experience the mighty power that raised him from the dead. I want to suffer with him, sharing in his death, so that one way or another I will experience the resurrection from the dead."**

In other words, she was saying that she wanted to know what God had in mind for her life, when he first created her. She was speaking of fulfilling her original "purpose." She wanted to know the real reason God first took hold of her life, from the very beginning. That's deep, isn't it? This is the mentality of a new breed. This is how Carmen thought, and I could hear it in many of the conversations we had over the years.

She spent much time in the presence of the Lord, arming and equipping herself with the spiritual weapons necessary to *"reign in life by Christ Jesus"* (Rom. 5:17). She had a *strength in the Spirit realm* that was so powerful to experience, anytime that you were blessed to be in her presence.

This type of strength is described in a verse in Daniel 11:32 (NASB), which says: *"But the people who know their God will display strength and take action."* They will not be backed up or denied even in the face of demonic opposition. Carmen actually saw herself as a member of a *counterculture* being raised up in the earth for the glory of God, to stand against an *antichrist system* that is filled with hatred, injustice, and much demonic activity.

Was she always this way? No, but over the years she grew, through the study of God's Word and the power of the Holy Spirit working together in her life. She came to understand these biblical principles of how the Christian life was designed to be lived.

She learned that this was the context in which ministry was designed to take place. She would often say, as Jesus said of Himself:

> **"The Spirit of the Lord is upon me. He hath anointed me to preach the gospel to the poor; he hath sent me to heal the broken hearted, to preach deliverance to**

the captives, and recover of sight to the blind, to set at liberty those who are bruised, and to preach the acceptable year of the Lord."

(Luke 4:18-19 KJV)

One of the key things that helped me to understand that Carmen was clearly a new breed, was when I read the part in my pastor's book on "The Emerging New Breed," where he gave a biblical profile of a new breed.

He said that "the New Breed is necessarily birthed in life threatening situations, i.e. crisis."[5]

He goes on to say:

"Crisis does not destroy these revolutionaries. To the contrary, they are probably at their best in a crisis. Even in biblical times crisis was what seemed to expose the true leaders of God more than anything else."[6]

Seeing Christ In the Crisis

This statement caused me to reflect once again on something Carmen said to me years ago, when she was in another crisis season in her life. She said the Lord talked to her about seeing "Christ in the Crisis."

You see, Carmen had experienced many crisis moments in her life. There was a time that she almost died once before from a physical challenge. It had us all rushing to the emergency room fighting for her life. Then, there was another time when she had serious eye surgery, and many, many other crisis moments along the journey of life. Somehow, by the grace of God, she learned to see Christ in the crisis, which always seemed

13

to "minimize" the size of her problem in her own eyes.

One of her many favorite verses was Psalms 34:3, where it says, *"Oh magnify the Lord with me and let us exalt His name together."* I learned from this (on reflection) that she had learned to "magnify" Him, which "minimized" everything else that presented a challenge for her. When she considered the sufferings of Christ and all that He endured on the cross to give us a new life in Him, it changed her perspective.

I think she saw what the scriptures meant where it says in Romans 8:18,

> **"For I reckon that the sufferings of this present time are not worthy to be compared with the glory that shall be revealed in us."**

She learned to keep her personal suffering in the *context* of Christ, and His sufferings for our sins. I think she must have understood Philippians 1:29 very well, where the apostle Paul says, *"For unto you it is given in the behalf of Christ, not only to believe on him, but also to suffer for his sake."* Did you hear that? It says to *believe* and to *suffer* for Christ sake. Carmen didn't want to suffer any more than anyone else does, but she was willing to pay that price as the Lord's representative in the earth. As she grew in her walk with Him, she learned that it was really not about her, but all about Him!

The reason I wanted to take time to share this with you is because this New Breed lifestyle is the life that we are **all** called to live. This was not a life that was intended to be "unique" to a few people in the earth, but actually the lifestyle that all believers are called to live in Christ Jesus. Someone may be thinking, but how do you really know if you are a new breed? Here are some of the key questions Bishop Charles L. Middleton Sr.

challenged us to reflect on, to see how we are progressing in this area from his new breed book:

- Have I been, in some sense, birthed or born in a life-threatening situation?
- Am I now in some kind of crisis?
- How am I handling it?
- Do I really know in whom I have believed?
- Do I discern His voice?
- Am I being tested in this area?
- What about my heart-felt convictions? Am I really convinced that God is who He says He is?
- Can He really do what He says He can do?
- What about me? Am I really a new creation?
- Is my lifestyle characterized by faith?
- Do I consistently "freak out" when I'm facing impossible situations?
- Do I sense that more and more what's important to me is doing the will of God?
- What's more important now? Preserving the old order? Walking in the newness of life?[7]

Then he goes on to say, "Don't be surprised if it turns out that you are (after all) a bonafide member of the Emerging New Breed."[8]

As I seek to squeeze out the nutrients of a life well lived as a new breed (from my covenant sister's life), I want to encourage you to seek to come up higher—in Him.

Who knew that she would have such a short time to come into these powerful revelations (and walk in them) so that she could leave her life as a legacy in the earth for the body of Christ? Let's all seek to make the time we have here on earth count for something.

Will it cost us something? Absolutely, it's a life laid down for the cause of Christ. Will it be worth it?

Absolutely, there is no better way to live than after the pattern of the sacrificial life that can be seen in Jesus Christ, as we seek to be conformed to His image. It's what life on earth is really all about.

We are called to represent Him at the highest level, by *knowing* Him and making Him *known* throughout the earth. God wants mankind to see what salvation looks like through us! He wants them to see His "power" to transform ordinary lives, which helps *unbelievers* to *believe* that He could do the same thing for them.

What an awesome assignment we have been entrusted with. If you have been slacking in this area of your life, why not stop right here for a moment and "recommit" your life to our Lord and Saviour, Jesus Christ, and to the task at hand! As my Pastor always says, *"It ain't too late to get it straight."* The Lord is waiting patiently just to hear from you—right now!

CHAPTER 3

THESE ALL DIED IN FAITH

"Now faith is the substance of things hoped for, the evidence of things not seen"

Hebrews 11:1

For we walk by faith, not by sight.

II Corinthians 5:7

Whatsoever is not of faith is sin.

Romans 14:23

I have fought the good fight, I have finished the race, I have kept the faith.

2 Timothy 4:7

I just cannot express how much I love the book of Hebrews, especially the 11th Chapter. It is sometimes referred to as the roll call of the heroes of faith. I have read this book several times in different translations, because I want to understand the depth of this kind of faith that is described in this chapter.

It's amazing to me to read about the kind of suffering these saints of old suffered through, without ever denying the faith. These old saints that have went before us kept their faith, confidence, and trust in God. One of the most amazing things to me from this 11th chapter is in verse 39 where it says *these all died in faith not having received the promise.*

Wow! That is deep in reflecting on how these powerful men and women of the faith did not actually get to see the "fulfillment" of the promises they believed God for, during their life time. However, this verse goes on to say,

> **"But having seen them afar off, and were persuaded of them, and embraced them, and confessed that they were strangers and pilgrims on the earth."**

Later on, in verse 40 of this same chapter, in Hebrews 11, we find out the reason these old saints could not receive the fulfillment of these promises in their lifetime. In the New Living Translation of this verse it says it like this:

> **"All these people earned a good reputation because of their faith, yet none of them received all that God had promised. For God had something better in mind for us, so that they would not reach perfection without us."**

Now that's a powerful biblical truth! They could not receive the promise without us, so they died in faith awaiting it! They had to wait on those of us yet to come, so we could come into the fulfillment of the promises of God—together! These saints were looking forward to a home yet to come in the heavenlies. It was to be a heavenly city prepared for the people of God called, *"a better country"* in the scriptures.

Looking Forward

After reading some of this text in the book of Hebrews, I think we can conclude that these saints understood clearly that this world was not their home.

Knowing this truth kept them looking forward to a home that was yet to come—with great expectation. Just like it says in Hebrews 13:14, *"For this world is not our permanent home; we are looking forward to a home yet to come."* This means, then, that they died in faith while waiting for the promises of God.

This may be a tough place for most of us, because we may feel it is unfair to wait for something, pray for it and believe God, but not receive the manifestation of it in our life time. I know what you mean. I kind of felt like that a little myself when Carmen passed, because I knew there were things she was still dreaming about doing and praying about too—not as much for herself but for our ministry, her family and friends, as well as the unsaved world, that she was not going to get to see with her own eyes. However, after reading this text again after her passing, I saw a different perspective.

When you have faith, you know deep within your heart that it's going to happen, whether it happens in your lifetime or not. Things like household salvation for example. You and I may not live to see all of our loved ones saved, but by faith we believe God will continue to draw them by His Spirit to himself, even after we are gone.

The beauty of it all is that our prayers (that we prayed in faith) are still at work even after we are gone. So, God will still honor them even after our death; because he honors his Word. Some of us are still being covered from the hand of our enemy (satan), right now, off of the prayers of faith that our grandmothers (or "big mama," as we use to call them) prayed in the past. Also, the prayers of our fathers and mothers, and many others who have prayed for God to bless and keep us over the years. These old saints have been long gone to their eternal home.

However, since God always hears the cry of the righteous because of his faithfulness (Ps. 34:17), He is still honouring those prayers, thank God! These old saints are now all a part of what is called "The Great Cloud of Witnesses." They are in the grandstands of heaven, cheering us on to the finish line of the faith journey. They are encouraging us to finish the race set before us. They have passed the baton on to us, that we might run with a spirit of perseverance! The bible says it like this in Hebrews 12:1 (NIV), after sharing with us the roll call of these heroes of the faith:

> "Therefore, since we are surrounded by a great cloud of witnesses, let us lay aside every weight and the sin that clings so closely, and let us run with perseverance the race that is set before us looking unto Jesus the pioneer and perfector of our faith."

How did they make it? It was by faith. How will we make it? By "looking unto Jesus, who is the pioneer and perfector of our faith." It was all by faith. In another one of Bishop Middleton's books on faith called, *The Life That Pleases God*, he says this regarding faith:

> "This confidence and trust in God is a matter of the heart (the human spirit). This same disposition of the heart is also referred to as "inner certainty" or being "fully persuaded" or "thoroughly assured" all these terms mean the same thing."[9]

It is the kind of faith that Abraham had, when he did not consider the deadness of Sarah's womb or the deadness of his own body (Rom. 4:19).

When all their natural ability was gone to produce a child, he believed that God could and would fulfil the promise he had made to give them a child in their old age, and God pulled it off too, all by Himself!

Isaac, the promised child did show up on the scene which was a miracle. Abraham, had that "inner certainty" that Bishop just talked about from his book. However, not all promises of God turn out this way in our life time, for reasons that may be unknown to us.

Many of the saints of old didn't get to see with their own eyes all of the fulfillment of the promises God made to them, but they still believed right up to the very end!

Believe me, I know it would be wonderful to live to see all these things happen in our lifetime, but it is even better, I think, to die with *"the full assurance of faith"* in the faithfulness of God. Because faith is now, therefore we believe we receive *when* we pray! Now that is the meaning of real biblical faith! You must have *faith* and *hope* in order to maintain this kind of posture of — stability. That's because faith is now, but hope is futuristic. Hope is "expectation." Therefore, we must keep expecting an amazing outcome when all is said and done. Hope, then, will keep you stable through the process!

In thinking about God still honouring our prayers after we are gone from the earth, reminds me of a time when Carmen and I were walking around the community of our church together. We were in the midst of declaring that all those abandon apartment buildings around our church, would be full of people that God would draw by his Spirit, to our church home. We always prayed that they would be healed, delivered, and receive Jesus Christ as their personal Lord and Saviour, and go on to live the life that pleases God.

While we were walking the streets on that day, Carmen looked up at those abandon buildings and said, *"Ron, long after we are gone God, will still be honouring the prayers that we have prayed over this community."* Isn't that something?

Although things in our community looked dry, abandoned and unfruitful, she saw something through the eyes of faith. She saw that our prayers were being planted as little seeds in the ground, that would one day come up and produce a mighty harvest in the earth. Even if it didn't happen until we were gone.

She actually saw the faithfulness of God in the realm of the Spirit! Our faith posture has to be expressed or released in some way, whether we see any natural evidence of what we believe for or not. Faith must precede the manifestation or it would not be faith, would it?

We praise and thank God right now because we know by faith that we already have it. The bible says in Hebrews 11:1, *"Now faith is the substance of things hoped for the evidence of things not seen."* Sometimes it's a sacrifice to praise God when it looks like things are not going to turn out like we thought or desired. When the "natural truth" is sending you a strong message, that it's not going to be fulfilled in your lifetime.

Can you still praise God through the eyes of faith? Yes, you can! You just lift your hands and open your mouth in praise to the Lord, *not* because you feel like it, but you do it by faith. Actually, we are told to make a continual sacrifice of praise to God. We can do this even in times of grief.

It says it like this in Hebrews 13:15 (NLT),

"Therefore, let us offer through Jesus a continual sacrifice of praise to God, proclaiming our allegiance to his name. And don't forget to do good and to share with those in need. These are the sacrifices that please God."

I Pledge Allegiance

This is part of our "allegiance" to his name according to this verse where it says *"proclaiming our allegiance."* Our allegiance has to do with our "loyalty" and our "commitment" to Him, which is to be proclaimed out of our mouths! How do we proclaim our spiritual allegiance to Jesus' Name? It's through the "continual" sacrifice of praise to God. In order to make a *sacrifice* you and I must understand that it's going to be costly.

It will certainly not be convenient either. It will require you to do it even when you do not feel like it. You do it because you know He is worthy of it in spite of how you feel or how bad your situation seems to be. You override these things to declare his worth. You do it through tears and pain, sorrow, sadness, and the grief you feel in the loss of your loved one. Although your circumstances have now changed, you know in your heart that you serve the one who remains the same. *"Jesus Christ the same yesterday, today, and forever more"* (Hebrews 13:8).

Why am I saying all of this to you, you might be thinking? It's because I want to encourage you to stay in faith, even though I know that you are deeply hurt about your loved one not getting to reach the point of "fulfillment" of certain things. They may have even shared some things with you that they believed would happen in their lifetime. However, as time goes by, you will see that some of the things that they declared in faith will still come to pass, and you will be so amazed when they do.

I am delighted to say that I've been seeing the fulfillment of some of those things, since Carmen passed away. When I see certain manifestations of what was on her heart, I just smile within myself and say, Wow! What a mighty God we serve.

It's is absolutely awesome to see how God is yet honouring His Word and her prayers! He's so faithful! Now, I want to ask you if you have fulfilled your "Pledge of Allegiance" today? Remember, your pledge of allegiance is your continual sacrifice of praise to Him, even in the midst of your pain. Remember, the Bible says in Psalms 34:1, *"I will bless the Lord at all times..."*. So, why not step out right now by faith and give God a worthy praise right in the midst of it all!

He will be waiting to meet you in the praise and to break every chain off your life, as only He can!

CHAPTER 4

─────────〜─────────

WHERE DO WE GO FROM HERE?

"I know the thoughts that I think of you saith the Lord, thoughts of peace and not of evil to give you a hope and a future."

Jeremiah 29:11

Why art thou cast down, O my soul? And why art thou disquieted within me? Hope in God. For I shall yet praise him, who is the health of my countenance, and my God.

Psalm 43:5

Once someone you loved so much goes home to be with the Lord, you may begin to feel like you no longer have a strong sense of direction for your life. You might say it feels like a bit of a wilderness experience. However, thank God that it is just a "feeling" and not necessarily the way it is in reality—from God's perspective.

It may be the passing of a husband, wife, son or daughter, sister or a brother. It may even be a grandparent, a baby or perhaps a very dear friend that brings on this type of "cast down" feeling in your soul. One reason this happens is because so much of your life was wrapped up in theirs, over the years. You had become "one" with them and connected in a very real and vital relationship.

Since death can be defined as *separation,* you will feel some sense of loss of the oneness you had with them. This can happen no matter how short the time frame was that they were a part of your life. During the actual planning of the funeral and making all the arrangements, you were probably so busy that you may not have felt this way at first. You may be still in such a state of shock, that you really do not know the depth of how you really feel on the inside. Sometimes it doesn't all come crashing down on you until it's all over. It might depend on what the circumstances were of their passing too, especially if it were a sudden death or from a tragic accident, which can send even deeper shockwaves through your system.

However, after the funeral is over and you have a chance to quiet down, you may find yourself asking questions like—*so where do I go from here?* I felt the same way too in the passing of my beloved sister in Christ, Carmen. Her life had become so intertwined with mine, that once she was gone from this expression of life, I almost felt like I was wandering aimlessly around grasping for a clear sense of direction in where to go from here.

Deep down inside of me (in my spirit), I knew God still had a plan. It was still somewhat of a wilderness experience momentarily, for sure, but somehow, I still knew I would overcome these feelings by God's grace. I knew He would carry me through. He had done it before in the passing of both of my parents, so I was sure He would do it again! I just had to put all my trust and confidence in Him!

There was also something else that helped me through this wilderness wandering as well. It was something very precious that God had connected me to, for most of my life.

I had been raised in the church pretty much all my life, thanks to my parents. Sometimes, I think to myself when I look back on it all, *"what would I have done without the people of God!"*

Thank God that I was attached to a good church home with loving saints, in the midst of this process. God used the local church to help me through this part of my journey. I felt somewhat numb, and confused that the outcome of her life on earth had not turned out as her mother, sister, and I, along with so many other loved ones, had prayed for and hoped for.

Thank God that these emotions are only a feeling and, because they are feelings, they tend to come and go. The one who created us knows all things. He always knows what our next step is after a devastating event has occurred in our lives. He is never without a plan no matter what the circumstances are that we have found ourselves in. As Carmen used to say to me all the time, *"Ron, nothing catches God by surprise!"*

Jeremiah 29:11 was one of Carmen's most favorite scriptures, and sometimes when she wanted to be a blessing to others (especially those in her church home) she would send a greeting card and write this text inside of it, with a happy face to top it off! I have countless cards and notes full of these greetings that she sent to me over the years! I think she obtained a powerful revelation of God's big plans for our lives when he revealed this text to her. It was an encouragement to her along the journey of life, and she unselfishly passed it on to all of us who knew her, to encourage us as well. She understood that God's "big plan" was not only for this life, but also for the life to come! Sometimes things happen in our lives that send shockwaves to our system, and life as we once knew it seems to no longer exist.

Though we may feel like we have been knocked off our feet momentarily, we must get back up by the grace of God. You see the truth is that God never intended us to live our lives out aimlessly here, as we journey through life with Him. Life on earth is too short to live it without "purpose" and "intentionality."

God is an "intentional" God, so he always has a next place for us in Him, so he moves us along each day by His Spirit. He will let us take moments like this to catch our breath (as we go through the grieving process), but then he will soon start to move us along again, just like He did with the children of Israel who were moving with the cloud as they traveled through the wilderness on their way to the promised land (Exodus 13:21-22). They had times of rest and refreshment, but then they had to pack up again and keep it moving, because they had not reached their destination yet.

God did the same thing for Elijah when he was in a place of discouragement over a life-threatening message from Jezebel. He had just had a major mountaintop experience of victory, which is usually when discouragement comes. He went into the wilderness and set up under a juniper tree in this sad state. It was in this place that Elijah, being so discouraged, prayed to die. God, in his love for him, sent an angel to awaken him, and encouraged him to arise and to eat—twice—so he could complete his journey and assignment in the earth. Then he went in the strength of what he had eaten supernaturally for forty days and forty nights. Later, God dealt with him and instructed him in the completion of his assignment, and he was able to move on from there (I Kings 19). It is the Holy Spirit who has the assignment to move us along as we "yield" ourselves to Him.

He will guide us into all truth, the truth about every aspect of our lives in Christ (John 16:13). He lives within us to guide, direct, counsel, feed, comfort and encourage us to keep on keeping on. The Holy Spirit is our "helper" that helps us to overcome the barriers, challenges, and the demonic attacks that come against our minds to bring discouragement, depression, fear, and torment.

When tough things occur in our lives just like when we are grieving, He is right alongside of us to see us through. He will help us with whatever season we may be in at the time. Thank God for sending the help of the Holy Spirit. What would we do without this "divine helper" living within our born-again spirit? However, we must remember that receiving this help does not automatically happen, though He is always *available* and *ready* to help us at any given moment. His ministry is released this way all the time. What I mean by that is, His ministry is more effectively released as we acknowledge our need for help, by something as simple as "asking" for it. It's as simple as that!

We must ask God to help us learn the simple discipline of sitting quietly in His presence, in seasons like this. We desperately need to listen for His voice to speak wonderful words of life into our born-again spirit. His words "*are spirit, and they are life*" (John 6:63). They produce the life of God within us that help to motivate us to never give up. It may now be a rather dry season for you because of the passing of your loved one, so you need to take it to Him in prayer. This is what is called drawing near to the Lord, and He said that if we draw near unto Him, then He would draw near unto us (James 4:8).

During this time of prayer and reflection, I want to encourage you to tell the Lord the truth about how you really feel. You may say things like, *"I feel abandoned, depressed or discouraged."* You do not have to pretend to be strong in His presence, for you are coming to the one who is the strength of your life (Ps. 27:1).

You may try to put on that strong face for others (to try to keep them from knowing the depth of your pain), but not in His presence. Why do that, since He already knows where you are at, spiritually, emotionally, physically and all? I know you don't think He's going to be shocked that you feel this way, do you?

God knows everything about us, so we cannot hide anything from Him anyway (Heb. 4:13). He created us, so who could know us any better than our very own creator? Just tell him the truth, He can handle it! He wants to illuminate your darkness (Ps. 18:28), and restore your soul when you come to Him (Ps. 23).

The bible encourages us to pour out our hearts before Him. It's okay to say, *"I'm hurt, I'm angry, I'm frustrated, I am disappointed, or how could you let this happen?* You aren't being disrespectful to say these things before your Creator. you are just telling God the truth about how you feel. He won't be angry with you for these expressions, because it's all just a part of being in a covenant relationship with God through Jesus Christ.

It's also a way of letting him know that you need his help in this situation. It's really a cry for help! It's a way of getting off the weight of the burden of trying to carry how you feel by yourself. I assure you that God will pour out in return his love, mercy and compassion upon you. The bible actually says,

"But you, O Lord, are a God of compassion and mercy, slow to get angry and filled with unfailing love and faithfulness."

Psalm 86:15 NLT

You are not going to catch Him by surprise with this outpouring of emotions, since he already knows they exist anyway. In fact, He is the one who created us with emotions in the first place, right?

Then guess what will probably happen next? He will adjust your thinking at some point and bring you powerful insights into another perspective of your situation. He will comfort you as only He can because he is *"the God of all Comfort"* (2 Cor. 1:3-5). He just may answer back with a little tough love like he did with Job when he was in a miserable state from all the bad stuff that had happened to him. Having lost pretty much everything, including his children and possessions, Job had a few good questions for God too! At first God seemed to be silent but then when God did answer back he told Job, *"where were you when I laid the foundations of the earth..."* (Job 38:4).

I Won't Complain

God opened up some serious revelations to Job about Himself, that made Job say (after he heard some of the revelations), *"Behold I am vile; what shall I answer thee? I will lay my hand upon my mouth (Job 40:4)."* I know this sounds tight, but it's right, and it is an act of the love of God to broaden our perspective of Him. Sometimes, we just need some fresh insights into who this awesome God is that we serve, in the midst of pouring out our list of complaints.

A fresh perspective of who God is will help us make the transition—from complaining to I won't complain—and that would be a good thing! We all remember the trouble Israel got into for all the complaining they did as they journeyed through the wilderness, on their way to the promised land. They went a little too far with their complaints and ended up wandering around in the wilderness for far too many years, and therefore, most of them did not make it into the promised land!

Before we reach that point, we may just need to say like Job did, *"I will lay my hand upon my mouth,"* when we are in the presence of the Lord, so that we don't go too far. We must learn where the boundaries are even when we are upset and do not understand the God we serve. So, what should we do then? We can come to Him and tell Him how we feel, but then be willing to be open and "listen" to his response and be willing to accept what He says back to us, like it or not!

God may just choose to use this time between you and himself to reveal who he is in truth just as he did with Job. I would encourage you to read this powerful Old Testament book of Job in the bible, if this is the frame of mind you have found yourself in these days. This book will really inspire you, especially when you get to the end of the book of Job.

Wait until you see how his latter days turned out. It was so much better than his former days. That's when God restored him in an absolutely amazing way! He got double for his trouble, and you will too. Why? Because God is always faithful!

I poured out a few of my own complaints as well, when He allowed Carmen to pass from this expression of life.

Then I remembered a scripture in Psalm 142:2 where King David said,

> **"I poured out my complaint before him;
> I showed before him my trouble. When
> my spirit was overwhelmed within me,
> then thou knewest my path..."**

God knew the path that David was on when his heart was overwhelmed by the circumstances and the challenges. Not taking place so much *outside* of him, but on the *inside* of him, that was the place of warfare! God knows what is going on *inside* of us, but he still wants us to communicate with him so he can comfort us, and even show us a biblical way of escape (I Cor. 10:13).

God knows and cares about the pain we feel and the heartache of it all. He can be touched with the feelings of our infirmities (Hebrews 4:15). You will experience what I am saying during this time of sorrow for sure, if you are willing to reach out to Him for help! He is fully prepared to rescue you! He is able to comfort us in *all* our tribulation if we are willing to receive His comfort with open arms.

I understand only too well the meaning of this verse on comfort from 2 Corinthians 1:4, because I have now received the Lord's comfort concerning my friend. I purpose to continue to receive it on a daily basis, since being comforted is not a one-time event. I especially need it when I am having one of those difficult days as well.

Sometimes when I look at a picture that I have on my desk of us sitting together at a luncheon, I have one of those difficult moments in time. This is the very reason I can now write this book to you to encourage you during your time of sorrow. It's because I can identify with your pain to some degree. However, I do want you to remember in the midst of it all that we, as believers, do not sorrow as those who have no hope according to I Thessalonians 4:13, which says:

> **"But I would not have you to be ignorant, brethren, concerning them which are asleep, that ye sorrow not, even as others which have no hope, for if we believe that Jesus died and rose again, even so them also which sleep in Jesus will God bring with him..."**

So, remember to sorrow *not* as though there is no hope of being together with them once again, at the appointed time. Until then, occupy until He comes (Luke 19:13)! Serve out your purpose for still being here in the earth. If you don't know what that is, just ask your heavenly Father. He can hardly wait to share it with you.

CHAPTER 5

"IN THE MEAN TIME..."

"...to be absent from the body and to be present with the Lord"

2 Corinthians 5:8-9

... And he called his ten servants and delivered them ten pounds, and said to them, occupy until I come."

Luke 19:13

Those of us who have loved ones who are gone home to be with the Lord often feel such an unexplainable absence of their *presence* in our daily lives. Every single day we may find ourselves thinking about their smile, that unforgettable hilarious laugh, or other funny ways in which they expressed themselves! Sometimes it was their unique sense of humor or just their presence around the house that stand out in our minds.

For others, it might be those special private conversations we had with them over the years. Not to mention the places we use to hang out with them on the weekends, like dining out at that favorite restaurant and eating a hot delicious meal together. Maybe it was a good workout with them at the gym, while you were both trying to work off those extra pounds that were clinging on for dear life.

At other times, we might find ourselves reflecting on the time we spent together on a fun-filled trip. It's true, isn't it, that we all have our own set of precious memories. Wow! How much life as we once knew it has changed! It seems that no area of life has been untouched by their absence.

Sometimes we might find ourselves wondering how we will ever adapt or be able to move on with life in a healthy, balanced way. After all, you never know what it's going to be like without them in this expression of life—until it actually happens. Not only that, but you certainly can't plan for it either—because you won't know the depth of the impact it will have on your life until it's over. It's all so strange and new.

It's tough when you have invested your life into the life of another, perhaps for years—especially like in marriage, or in the raising of children that you once did together as a couple. It can be frightening to think about being left to raise them alone. Who knew it would turn out this way, other than God, that is? Is there any good news in the midst of all of this, you might be wondering?

Believe it or not, yes there is! Remember, that there is a family in heaven and a family in the earth (Eph. 3:15). So, the good news in the midst of this is that you will see them again. That is, for those who knew the Lord Jesus Christ as their personal Lord and Savior, having received Him by faith. There is a home in heaven that awaits all of us who believe (2 Cor. 5:1). How awesome it will be when you *reunite* with them in the presence of the Lord, and live together with them throughout eternity—never to be separated again! Praise God, that's certainly something to look forward to. However, you might be wondering what you are going to do with yourself in the meantime, since you are still here upon the earth without them.

Although I don't have all the answers to this question of interest (for all who are experiencing the pain of grief), I do feel God has given me some "timely tips" to get you through the process! I'm sure that as you choose to spend quality time in the presence of *"the God of all comfort"* that He will reveal even more timely tips to help you along the way! These timely tips have been turned into a twenty-one-day breakthrough plan to help you break out of those narrow places into a broad place—in Him! Just take one a day in your personal time with Him. Look up the scripture reference that goes with it, and meditate on it, then practice being a doer of the Word!

Timely Tips: A 21 Day Breakthrough Plan!

1. **KNOW** that Jesus knows how you feel, he can be touched with the feelings of your infirmities (weaknesses), (Hebrews 4:15).
2. **BE STILL** and know that He is God (Psalms 46:10). In quietness and confidence will be your strength (Is. 30:15). Wait on the Lord and he will strengthen your heart (Psalms 27:14).
3. **SPEND TIME** in His presence. You have a personal relationship with Him. He wants to talk to you, and He wants you to listen. You don't always have to have something to say, just sit there and let him heal you of your wounds (Ps. 147:3).
4. **LISTEN** to music of comfort and joy to saturate your atmosphere with His LOVE. You can even sing your own song to the Lord. Ps. 95:1; Ex. 15:1; Ps. 101:1; Ps. 150:1-5; Col. 3:16.Ps. 57:7.
5. **REST ASSURED** that God still has a plan for your life; that's why he's still holding your soul in life (Ps. 66:9). He knows the plans... (Jeremiah 29:11).

6. **GRIEVE** but do not sorrow as those who have no hope. I Thessalonians 4:13; John 16:22. God gives us *permission* and a *period* of time to grieve! (**Read:** Deuteronomy 34:9). Ask God "is my time period up?"

7. **TAKE EVERYTHING** to God in prayer. He can handle it! Tell him how you really feel since you can't hide anything from him anyway! *"God I am angry, I'm confused, how could you let this happen?"* Philippians 4:6 says, "In everything by prayer and supplication with thanksgiving let your request be made known unto God...".

8. **BE OKAY** with having some *unanswered* questions. That's what it really means to trust God with all your heart. We will understand it better by and by. Rest in His Sovereignty, He is the only wise God! (Proverbs 3:5-6). Now we see through a glass darkly (I Corinthians 13:12).

9. **RECEIVE** the Lord's comfort. He is the God of all comfort (2 Corinthians 1:3-4). Also, be open to letting other's comfort you; they are God's hands extended to you in your time of need.

10. **HOLD ON** to those precious memories. No one can take those away from you! Ask God to bring back to you some good memories you may have forgotten! 2 Tim. 1:5-14. Read it also from The Message bible. One precious memory may trigger another.

11. **DO** what you once loved to do when your loved one was still with you, i.e., go out to dinner, travel, or go to a movie. They would want you to still have some FUN! John 10:10.

12. **DO NOT** forsake the assembly of the saints. (Hebrews 10:25, 26). You may not feel up to it every single Sunday, but ask for God's grace to help you to go anyway. Being in the *fellowship* and atmosphere of the saints is so helpful in getting through the grieving process.

We are a spiritual family (called the body of Christ), which makes us members of one another assigned to build each other up. Also, you need a word in season to help you through the process! (Proverbs 12:25; Proverbs 15:23).

13. **DO NOT** hide yourself from your own flesh (Isaiah 58:7b) Do not shut out your other natural family members because of your personal pain. They are in pain, too. Learn how to comfort one another through the process. You need each other even more now. Guard against isolation! It's a trick of the enemy to pick you off by deepening the depression, and leading you into despair and a place of hopelessness.

14. **FIND** something to do to bless others. These acts of "kindness" will help you to get your mind off of yourself and your pain. Reach out to those who are sick or grieving, as well as those who are celebrating a special occasion in their life. It will help lift your spirits too! You can even look up some volunteer organizations like the Red Cross. There are so many others that need help too. You could even volunteer at your church as well!

15. **CALL** upon the name of the Lord! Just say **JESUS** when you are in unexplainable pain, and His presence will show up every time, to bring deliverance and healing for your soul! He heals the brokenhearted (Luke 4:18). He's so faithful!

16. **READ** your bible even when you don't feel like it. God will lift your spirits through his Word. His words are Spirit and they are life (John 6:63). They will bring rejoicing to your heart. (Jeremiah 15:16).

17. **PRAISE GOD** for the gift you had in your loved one. Thank Him for the time you did have with them, and the impact they had on your life. Thank God that they were saved and are in the

awesome presence of the Lord, I Thessalonians 5:18; Psalm 136.

18. **LIVE!** Don't just exist. You were not created to be a robot! You are still filled with the life of God. You are a gift to this world and you still have so much to give. Jesus came that we might have life and that more abundantly (John 10:10). Confess and verbally declare that you will live and not die and declare the works of the Lord (Ps. 118:17). You must fulfil your assignment in the earth. Be open, be flexible. Let him stretch you out of your comfort zone! Don't be afraid to try something new. Fear not! Psalm 56:3.

19. **KNOW** that the **JOY** of the Lord is your strength. Rejoice even when you don't feel like it. Put on the garment of praise for the spirit of heaviness (Isaiah 61:1-3).

20. **TAKE** one day at a time! Don't try to plan too far out in the future about how you will make it through this season; just take it—ONE DAY AT A TIME. Matt.6:34.

21. **KNOW** that this too shall pass! It won't always feel like this; things will get better. It's a process. Never give up—JESUS will carry you through the journey, he will see you through! Heb. 13:5-6.

Note: Reflect back on these from time to time to help you continue to get breakthroughs—through those narrow places.

CHAPTER 6

PRECIOUS MEMORIES

"Verily I say unto you, Wheresoever this gospel shall be preached in the whole world, there shall also this, that this woman hath done, be told for a memorial of her."

Matt. 26:13

"...he said unto his disciples gather up the fragments that remain, that nothing be lost."

John 6:12

What a blessing it is, after all is said and done, to know that all is not lost, since you and I still have our—precious memories. These are what might be termed the 'leftovers' after our loved ones have passed on. Have you ever had a delicious meal and had some leftovers? If you have, then you know that there is nothing like the leftovers! They are absolutely delicious! You just warm them up the next day and eat them all up, licking your lips all along the way!

When Jesus had finished feeding a multitude of folks, He told the disciples to *"gather up those fragments that remain that nothing be lost."* We can do the same thing, too, by feeding off the precious memories of the lives of our loved ones. After all, we do still have something left, don't we?

When God created us, He gave us a wonderful capacity (among many other things), and that is to be able to *remember*. When we suffer loss, satan would have us to reflect, focus on and torment ourselves over the depth of our losses. This is the nature of the "battlefield" of the mind. Sometimes we will find ourselves going over and over again in our minds about how different our life will be now without them, and the pain of it all. However, since we have something to say about what we meditate on, then we know that we can make a *choice* to think on the good things.

Philippians 4:8 (AMP) tells us to think on:

"...whatever is true, whatever is worthy of reverence and is honorable and seemly, whatever is just, whatever is pure, whatever is lovely and lovable, whatever is kind and winsome and gracious, if there is any virtue and excellence, if there is anything worthy of praise, think on and weigh and take account of these things (fix your minds on them)."

It all amounts to a "choice," doesn't it? If you choose to think on the negative things or all the bad things that happened in the life of your loved one, it will only lead to discouragement. Then, if left unchecked, it will move on to depression and a downward spiral that may end up taking you years to recover from. However, if you *choose life* (which is to think on the good things), then it will produce life in you (Deut. 30:19).

You just may end up finding yourself laughing at some of the memories, or thinking about all the good things you learned from them. It may be some of those fun events that you were both involved in together that make such happy memories. This will lift your spirits and you will begin to feel some better.

You may even cry some during the process as you reflect on those memories, and that's okay too. It's all a part of the journey. Ultimately, you will be alright after all is said and done.

As I began to reflect back on the good things about my precious friend, Carmen, my heart began to rejoice! I experienced a range of emotions and as I began to write them down, it brought laughter and healing to my soul. She was such fun just to be around. It was never a dull moment, believe me! So, I thought I would take time out to share some of my precious memories with you. As a little joke among her family members and friends, we all seemed to agree that Carmen just may have missed her calling to be a *comedian* rather than a social worker. That was because she could always keep you laughing.

Some of the things I will share with you may get a little laugh out of you, or at least a smile to help brighten up your day. You may even end up saying *Wow! My loved one was the same way.* I'm so excited about sharing these things not only with you, the reader, but with her family members and other friends as well, for she had many of them. They will be well able to identify with some of the things I am about to share with you.

I hope as I share so many wonderful things about my precious friend, that you will not get the impression that she was *perfect.* None of us have arrived yet for sure. However, she was a different kind of Christian as you will soon see. It was because she loved God so much and longed to live the life that pleases Him (Rev. 4:11). I hope you will enjoy this moment of sharing straight from the heart! Let's lighten up, and have a little fun as I reflect on some very precious memories of a life well lived.

Sharing Precious Memories

> ➢ Carmen the comedian always had a sense of humour even in the worst situations. Just when you wanted to cry and were near tears, she would say something funny, and you would end of laughing instead of crying.

> ➢ Always greeting you with a warm smile no matter what kind of day she was having herself. She made it all about you!

> ➢ Her laugh was infectious! You would start laughing with her even if nothing was funny. She had the pearliest white teeth and the brightest smile that would always brighten you up, even on your worst day!

> ➢ She would always say "thank you" over and over again (even for the smallest things), especially when she was sick. When you were leaving from a visit with her at the hospital she would say *"thank you,"* *"I appreciate you"*, *"I love you,"* more than once as you left out of the door. She never took her blessings for granted. She was so glad that God had blessed her to have people in her life who really loved and cared for her.

> ➢ I loved this one. Whenever we had been out together somewhere and she would drop me off, she would blow the horn twice as she pulled off. I got so use to it that if she forgot to do it I would mention it, and we would laugh.

> ➢ She would offer you a ride home even if you could see that the car had reached its full capacity. The saints would be sitting in there like sardines in a can. Then she would say, *"Come on Ron,"* and I would start laughing, thinking to myself, *"Hmm,*

Now where am I going to sit?" She would still say, *"Come on. I will take you home."* She was never willing to leave anyone stranded, no matter how far away you lived.

➢ She would always remember the special occasions in your life, rarely going anywhere without a gift. If she couldn't come to your event, she would send a card (with money enclosed). Then she would call you, or pray for you on the phone to let you know that she was celebrating your special day with you. She would pray a powerful prayer over your life (that you would have a blessed day) before she hung up the phone.

➢ I remember several times when I was sick and she would come by and bring juice, water or whatever she thought would help me to get well.

➢ If you bought her something she would act like you just gave her a million dollars! Her eyes would light up like a little child receiving a gift at Christmas time.

➢ If you were saying something to her that she knew was not the right attitude, she would hear you out first, as you stated your case. She was always such a good listener, so she would be as quiet as a mouse, then she would say, *"Now, I don't mean no harm Ron, but that's not God."*

➢ She was always able to give you a fresh biblical perspective of your problem, and she was the most confidential person I have ever known.

> ➤ She was a peacemaker. She learned to walk in the peace of God, and help others to come to a place of peace with their brothers and sisters in Christ. She had a gift for bringing people together during the worst of times. She knew how *not* to take sides in order to be fair, and bring about reconciliation when conflict arose. She was serious about peacemaking!
> ➤ She knew how to love you unconditionally. She knew you had flaws and weaknesses just like she did, so she always extended "mercy" to you.
> ➤ When you were in her car and a song would come on that she knew you liked, she would say, *"Now this song is going out to none other than Rhonda R. Roberson."* Then, she would name the song and start laughing. She would make such an event out of that moment!
> ➤ I miss sitting together with her in church and watching her get her praise on in the dance, dancing at least 100 miles per hour (I'm exaggerating a little bit, but not much).
> ➤ I loved the way her eyes would light up when she would get a fresh revelation from the scriptures. She would be so excited. She just loved the Word of God and we loved sharing our revelations together on the phone.
> ➤ If you were around her for even a moment, you were going to leave encouraged. She would have a word in season for the weary or a good warm hug always. The love of God was shed abroad in her heart by the Holy Spirit (Rom. 5:5).

➢ She loved a good meal. She loved going out to dinner and eating delicious food with family and friends, especially desserts!

➢ She had a special knack for being able to get you to do just about anything within reason. She was always rallying people together to support a cause that God had placed on her heart!

➢ I loved how serious she was about everybody having a bible. She would buy you a bible and have your name engraved on it. She did this for her relatives, friends, and neighbors as well. She also worked with me in community outreach so she would purchase cases of bibles for our new members, and people from the community as well. She understood the power and the authority of God's Word and how life-changing it was to know the Word of God.

➢ Last but not least, I loved the way she loved her family. She understood that family was important. It was a joy to experience firsthand how much she loved her mother and sister. There was nothing she wouldn't do to be a blessing to them. They had good times, bad times, happy and sad times too, but they always stuck it out together by the grace of God.

➢ Just one more thing I must say about my friend right here. She was by far one of the most powerful intercessors in the earth, that I have ever known. She understood the power of prayer and was willing to pay the price of standing in the gap. She knew how to tap into the very heart of God in prayer. She prayed prayers that *resonate* with the heart of God! She was fully persuaded that prayer works!

I could say so much more about her, but instead I will just say (with an acronym) that she was **PRECIOUS!**

Pleasing to the Father — she stood in awe of Him!

Respectful of everyone, whether she knew you or not.

Encouraging others to be the best they could be.

Compassionate and sensitive to the needs of others.

In consistent prayer for others to get a breakthrough in life.

Outstanding friend; she was truly one of a kind.

Unselfish — always putting the needs of others first.

Soooo thoughtful — always ready to lend a helping hand.

Precious in the sight of the LORD is the death of his saints.

— Psalm 116:15 (Emphasis mine)

Now, I want to encourage you to take a moment and record a few precious memories of your loved one right here. Though all of your times together with your loved one may not have been so pleasant, you can always find something about everyone that was.

Remember, it may be things that made you laugh, time spent together, a trip you took out of town or just some funny ways that your loved one had of expressing themselves. Just write whatever comes to mind!

You may just find yourself laughing rather than crying at this point, and that would be a good thing—especially since the bible says *"a merry heart doeth good like a medicine"* (Proverbs 17:22). However, at the same time it is also okay to shed some tears, too, as you reflect upon your time with your precious loved one(s).

It is said of Christ in Hebrews 5:7,

> **"that in the days of his flesh, when he had offered up prayers and supplications with strong crying and tears unto him that was able to save him from death, and was heard in that he feared."**

Just know you have permission to cry as well, as you record those precious memories that have been tucked away in your heart.

Recording Precious Memories

_____
_____
_____
_____
_____
_____
_____
_____

_____
_____
_____
_____
_____
_____
_____
_____
_____
_____
_____
_____
_____
_____
_____
_____
_____
_____
_____
_____
_____
_____
_____
_____
_____
_____

Note: If you run out of space please continue writing in a notebook, some of the precious memories the Lord brings back to your remembrance. Just let it flow! Then from time to time, come back and read them just to encourage yourself.

CHAPTER 7

ANY REGRETS?

"Brethren, I count not myself to have apprehended; but this one thing I do, forgetting those things which are behind, and reaching forth, unto those things which are before, I press toward the mark for the prize of the high calling of God in Christ Jesus."

Philippians 3:13-14

For all have sinned and fallen short of the glory of God.

Romans 3:23

Regrets, regrets, regrets! What do you do with regrets when someone you loved so much is gone? You may have some regrets about things said, not said, or things you should have done, or things you didn't do! Well, I think I know what you mean! Actually, I have a few of them of my own. One of them I think I would like to share with you is about making biscuits. You see, I didn't have much of a history of being a cook as it was already. So most of my friends would look at me with a little *suspect* in their eyes if I said I cooked anything.

Carmen felt the same way about it too, since I had never cooked anything for her in times past. That's why there was a little joke between us about my cooking homemade biscuits like my mother used to make.

I knew I could do it, but I had no evidence to make myself credible in her eyes. I had done it with my mom many times before, but the question was—where was the proof?

For years, I would go out of town and visit my mom, and we would make biscuits together for breakfast a few times before I left. When I came back I would be so excited and pumped up about making some of them for Carmen, and my family as well. I would tell her that I was going make her some, but then after I had been back home for a while (the spirit of procrastination would overtake me), and I soon found my desire to make them, fizzling out.

I would look in the kitchen and find that I didn't seem to have all the ingredients I needed, and end up saying I would do it later, once I had a chance to go shopping for them. Sometimes she would mention those biscuits and we would laugh about it. Then I would say, *"I'm still going to make them for sure. I'm going to prove to you that I know how to make them."* Then she would say, *"Yeah, right"* and start laughing, then I would start laughing with her. However, as time continued to go by, I ended up never making them for her, and suddenly it was just too late.

Now, I know that this was not some extremely big deal in one way of looking at it, and certainly nothing to go on some long guilt trip about. After all, I know Carmen is not in heaven right now mad at me, and grieving over my not having made those biscuits for her, especially since she is now in the very awesome presence of the Lord. However, I felt the need to share this with you because when people pass from this life, most of us can think of several things we should have said or done, but now it's too late to say or do them. Although I didn't share all of my regrets with you, I still realize that some of you may have far deeper regrets than even I do.

So many people are suffering such intense pain on the inside for various reasons related to grieving. Some people were angry with loved ones, and had so many arguments about things you may now realize were "petty issues" as you reflect back on them. Others made promises of things they would do for their loved ones, which are now broken promises. Some never said I love you or didn't say it often enough, while others refused to forgive an offence that happened between them from some time ago. Now you may feel stuck, unable to move on with life because of situations like this.

This is why it can (at times like these) become even worse for some people, when they are attending the funeral of their loved one(s). Perhaps it's worse for them at this point for more reasons than one. They may fall out at the casket and scream and cry uncontrollably, and others may look on and think they are making a spectacle out of themselves. But, perhaps, what they don't know is that this reaction is happening because they are not only overwhelmed by "grief," but also by "regrets." They may be in serious distress over past events in their relationship with their loved one that never got a proper closure.

Although I do know that this is not the case for everyone, it is a very emotional time when you reflect back on something that you now have absolutely no power whatsoever to change—it's devastating indeed. Most people want to know, now that it's too late, what do you do?

Well, though I am no expert on this subject and I surely don't have all of the answers, I still want to share what I do know to help you get past this—sticking point. One important point (regarding the past) that we all will have to face sooner or later is that—it's over. We cannot turn back the hands of time.

There's no time machine we can get in and undo what has already been done, like they try to show us on television. We can't make everything alright by trying to live our lives back there. It's just over, as painful as that reality may be! So, what are we to do now?

We may have to face another "reality" at the same time. What reality is that? It's the reality that we have "fallen short" to some degree in our relationship with our loved one, which I know is going to be a tough one to face.

Falling Short

This issue of falling short makes me reflect back in scripture to Peter (one of Jesus' disciples) who fell short through "pride" (Luke 22:54-62). When he missed the mark, Jesus looked at him without saying a word. You see, Peter had a rather high opinion of himself and didn't seem to think he was capable of falling short. He said that he would never deny Jesus even though Jesus told him he would, before the cock would crow three times. Then when Peter did deny him, Jesus turned and looked at him, and Peter didn't say a word either but rather went out and wept bitterly.

I really don't think that the look Jesus gave Peter was meant to make him feel condemned or to make him feel guilty. After all, the Lord's purpose is never served through *condemnation* but through *restoration*. So, later on Jesus does restore him (after he had risen from the dead), and Peter went on to accomplish great things for the master. In Mark 16:7, the angel said to the women who came to the tomb after Jesus had risen, *"But go your way, tell his disciples and Peter that he goeth before you into Galilee."*

You see how the Lord had the angel to single out Peter by name, when he called for the disciples to meet him as the risen Savior in Galilee?

Why? I believe it was to let him know that he still loved him and had not rejected him from the call on his life. Jesus soon makes this even more clear to him in John 21:15-19. This is a must read.

Peter's pride just had to be taken down a few notches through this experience. He had to eat "humble pie" as all of us have had to do at some time or another! However, in restoration you are put back in your right place and your right condition. That's just what Jesus did for Peter; He restored him.

We see this same type of *compassion* Jesus showed to Peter in another story of restoration. This type of compassion was shown in how Jesus dealt with a woman who was caught in adultery, when everyone else had in mind to stone her to death. Jesus asked her where were her accusers (who had by this time left), because none of them could cast the first stone, in light of their own sins. Then Jesus said to her, *"neither do I condemn thee, go and sin no more."*

I'm just saying this to say that we all miss it at times in our humanity. Jesus is already well aware of our weaknesses for sure, far more than we are! Therefore, be comforted by Psalms 103:14 (NIV), which says, *"For he knows how we are formed, he remembers we are dust."* Thank God that He has a great memory!

Sometimes our expectations of ourselves are a little too high. We, as Christians, are moving toward perfection but for sure we have not arrived yet! Life is a journey that must be walked out day by day by the grace of God. You won't always get it right on this journey, but when you know "who you are in Christ" you will realize that you don't have to live in guilt and condemnation (Isa. 53). Remember, Jesus came to set us free, so why should we still be bound when the Lord has set us free (Gal. 5:1)?

Christ already bore our guilt and sorrow at the cross. We were *not* created to live our lives always feeling guilty about something, especially since Jesus shed his *blood* to deliver and cleanse us from guilt and shame. Never forget that we who believe in him, are now the righteousness of God in Christ Jesus (2 Corinthians 5:21). We are actually clothed in his righteousness, which means that we are in right standing with God through Jesus Christ. We are now "rightly related" to the God of the whole universe. That's amazing!

We all have some regrets about the past, but we cannot unpack and live back there once it's over. I am confident as well that our loved ones who really loved us wouldn't want us to either, if they really loved us. It's healthy to remember the good times, it's also healthy to look back and laugh at the funny times too, but other than that we must go forward by faith.

So, please feel free to give God your regrets and your pain. He can handle it, and He will lift that heavy burden and give you the oil of joy for mourning and the garment of praise for heaviness (Isa. 61:3). He will anoint you with the oil of gladness as only He can (Ps. 45:7). However, I must add that if there is some "repenting" that needs to be done because you fell short —by all means repent.

The Power and the Process of Repentance

The bible tells us that "the goodness of God leads us to repentance" in Romans 2:4. It also tells us that He will forgive us of our sins and cleanse us from all unrighteousness in I John 1:9, as I think I may have mentioned already. So, repentance is a good thing, even though we may not like to do it, since it tends to hurt our pride to admit wrongdoing. It still is a good thing because of its "cleansing effect" upon our hearts.

Repentance cleanses us from the things that led to our downfall, which may have been a sin of *omission* or a sin of *commission*. We may have omitted something that we should have done, or it may have been intentional sin, that we now sincerely regret.

Either way, it can all be cleansed through sincere repentance before a holy and loving God. Repentance has to do with a radical change of mind that leads to a change in behaviour. I like the way my pastor breaks down repentance in one of his foundation books, where he gives a four-fold process. This is what it says:

The Process of Repentance is fourfold:

1. Consideration of our ways

2. Sorrow for transgressions

3. Renunciation of old ways

4. Change of behaviour[10]

Sometimes people say they have repented, but it has not resulted in a change of behaviour, i.e., our conduct. Perhaps this is because we sometimes do not go through the "process" of repentance; starting with consideration of our ways. This could be at the root of why we can't seem to come to a point of real change. So, let's all go through the process, so that we don't have to go around this same mountain again and again! Let's seek to reach the point of "godly sorrow" rather than the "sorrow of the world," spoken of in 2 Corinthians 7:10-12. It's a must read, as well!

Then, after you have repented and been cleansed and forgiven, go ahead and get back in the press toward the mark of the high calling of God in Christ Jesus.

Let's keep going from faith to faith (Rom. 1:17). Let's thank God together that all of our sins are now under the blood of Jesus!

Therefore, we no longer have to live in the land of regrets! What a blessing and an opportunity for a fresh start!

It's Time to Let It Go

At this point I thought that I was going to close this chapter, but then I had an unexpected "thought-provoking" conversation with my daughter, Shartrese, about the subject of regrets. Here are a few of the high points that came out of that conversation.

While none of us can do anything about our past regrets, as I have just talked to you about, there is something we can do going forward with the rest of our relationships with those still living among us. We must do something to *strengthen* our relationships in the earth. Some of us have made promises that we have not kept of things we would do for someone.

Others may need make an effort to strengthen their relationships with others by giving a warm hug, saying some loving heartfelt words, buying a gift, sending a card or making a phone call. We need to take more time to let others know that we love them, and that they are important to us. Remember that it is the God-kind of love, which is unconditional!

Out of all of these things we need to do (so that we do not end up with regrets all the time), there is one that concerns me more than the rest. It is those who are "holding grudges" and deep seated resentment in their hearts, toward people who have "offended" them in some way. Some of these offences may be current and still fresh, and very tender to the touch. While others may have been attached to the past. Some people are even still fuming over something someone said or did to them that was long ago, and they have vowed never to "forgive" them for it. This is not a good idea and it is certainly not in line with God's way of doing things.

We have already been warned through the scriptures to be on high alert regarding offence. It says in Luke 17:1 that *"offence will come..."*. So, since we know that it is coming at some point in all our lives, then what should we do? We need to find a redemptive way from the scriptures in how to handle it—a way that will bring glory to God, and absolutely none to our flesh!

First of all, we should forgive just because it is the right thing to do, and we are commanded to forgive according to the scriptures (Matt. 6:15). Not because we feel like it, but rather because it is right or pleasing in God's sight.

What if something happened to them and you never get a chance to apologize, or make up in some way with them? Even if it was not your fault as you see it, you still need to be "reconciled" back to each other, and the scriptures do give us a biblical pattern of how it should be handled in Matthew 18:15-18. You must go to them "face to face" first, prepared to speak the truth in love (Eph. 4:15).

After seeking to do that (perhaps more than once and it does not work out), then you can feel a release to bring in another non-partial, *mature* believer to seek reconciliation between the two of you. Someone who will not take sides is preferable. If that is unsuccessful, after having made several attempts, I would strongly suggest that you take it to the leadership of the church to help resolve the issue between you. If they are unsuccessful, then the bible gives further instruction on handing that, too, in this same passage of scripture.

Having said all of this, the bottom line is still going to be that you must *choose* to let it go! If you need to have a peace conference with them or whatever you need to do to get it right, please do not procrastinate about taking action to restore these vital relationships.

Please remember: forgiving does not always mean that you are now going to be buddy-buddy with them, from this point on. You may have to move on if it was an unhealthy or abusive relationship of some type. However, this does not absorb you of your *responsibility* to forgive.

Sometimes we get too caught up in how we feel or how bad we have been treated, which can soon become a reason *not* to forgive from our perspective. Trust me, this kind of thinking is a major waste of the precious time we are being given to make things right! Why not just ask God for the grace to say I am sorry, at least for the part we played in the division if nothing else. Nothing but pride can keep us from this action step. Remember, God *"resists the proud but gives grace to the humble"* (James 4:6).

You just need to ask God for the grace to say those two meaningful words—I'm sorry, and say it in sincerity from your heart; expressing it in some way with your actions as well. You must forgive from you heart according to the scripture in Matthew 18:35, which is not based on a feeling but rather it is a *decision* you make in obedience to God.

Then, just let God handle the rest according to his infinite wisdom. He knows very well how to deal with the people He created, for sure. Even if they don't apologize or admit wrongdoing toward you, (trust me as one who has been in many of these situations), He can handle it!

If you want to learn more about this important topic of forgiveness, please see the advertisement of my first book, *Let's Stay Together,* in the back of this book. I pray it will be a great blessing in your life.

I also want to encourage you to take time to read one of my favorite biblical stories of Joseph and his brothers. This story begins in Genesis chapter 37.

This powerful story continues to unfold for several chapters. It will be worth the time you spend working through it. I guarantee you that it will give you a fresh and lifechanging perspective on the importance of forgiveness. It will teach you how to take the low road to new heights in Christ! Then, let's go on and put an end to living a life—full of regrets!

CHAPTER 8

YOUR TEARS...

"He will swallow up death in victory; and the Lord God will wipe away tears from off all faces..."

Isaiah 25:8

"...and God shall wipe away all tears from their eyes."

Rev. 7:17

One thing that stands out for me about my covenant sister, Carmen, is how much she would cry. It soon became a little joke among all of us that knew her, about how she would burst out in tears at the drop of a hat! Those tears would just come streaming down her face, sometimes catching us totally by surprise when we were in her presence.

One of her favorite songs that she loved to hear was called "Your Tears," which was sung by Bishop Paul S. Morton. Sometimes those tears flowed out of her passion for global ministry, which is at the very heart of God. At other times, her tears were a part of her crying out to God for him to have mercy on world conditions and injustices being done toward the people God created and loves.

She was also crying out for the unsaved world, including some of her family members who were not saved yet. She longed in her heart for people to come to know the God she served, through Jesus Christ. She did not want anyone to be lost and die in their sins (2 Pet. 3:9). She spent much time in private prayer regarding these and other causes.

At other times her tears were tears of sorrow, not just over her own trials and tribulations, but what other people she knew were going through. This would include her mother and sister (whom she loved with all of her heart), who had some physical challenges of their own as well.

I remember so many times when we were in intercessory prayer at church, how Carmen would take our prayer list from the bulletin and have us all crying out to God to see the manifestation of his healing power in the bodies of the saints. At other times, she was crying out for those who were grieving over the passing of their loved ones. She had such compassion for people that she knew how to laugh and to cry with you. She knew how to rejoice with them that rejoice and weep with those that weep, as we are instructed to do from the scriptures (Romans 12:15). I just loved that about her.

One time I was in California because my mother was sick unto death. She soon passed while I was still there. As soon as I called Carmen to tell her on the phone that my mom was gone, she began to cry with me, as the tears streamed down my eyes on the other end of the phone.

Though she couldn't see me or hug me while I was going through that painful experience (because of the physical distance that was between us), she still felt my pain.

She knew how much I loved my mother, and my father too. My father was already deceased by this time, which caused my mother and I to grow even closer over the years. The way Carmen cried with me, you would have thought it was her mother.

That's the way she was, then she began to pray for me through her tears. Nobody could pray quiet like she could with such sensitivity, compassion and power, all rolled into one! God's Word was hidden in her heart and when she would pray you could feel yokes being destroyed and burdens being removed off of your life. After she finished going before the throne of grace for me, I began to feel so much better.

Then I was able to get myself together to do what I needed to do from there. It's amazing how God will use people in some absolutely incredible ways to help us along the journey of life. He cares so much about us and therefore, he will cause others to extend their hands as his hands outstretched to us in our time of need. Would our heavenly Father think of doing anything less when he hears the cry of his children?

Crying is a wonderful way that God has given us to release our emotions. There is nothing wrong with crying, whether you are male or female. It's healthy to cry. In the scriptures, it is encouraged.

There are many examples of people who wept in the scriptures. Like Abraham did over Sarah when she died (Gen. 23:2). Like Jacob did, when he thought his son Joseph was dead, as reported to him by his sons (Gen. 37:35). Then there was David, who wept over the death of Absalom, one of his sons (2 Sam. 18:33). Also, like David and his men who wept when their wives and children were taken captive by their enemies (I Sam. 30:4). The mention of these people represents just a few who experienced grief on some level in the scriptures, though their circumstances may be varied.

Sometimes you have a build-up on the inside that needs a release when traumatic things have taken place in your life, or you are going through a devastating time. You also may need to cry when you are rejoicing over the good things that have happened in your life or the life of others. What a wonderful release either way! If we could not release these emotions, they would probably come out in some other way that may not be healthy for us or those around us.

Sometimes when family members or close friends pass away, the family argues and fights with one another, tearing each other down with cruel words and evil conduct because of the pain of it all. Some families even start fighting over the material things of the one who has passed. This is not the way it should be, and God is not pleased with this type of conduct. Families should be able to cry and grieve together as one unit.

Although we may all have our different feelings and perspectives (of what we are going through during this difficult time), we must remember that we are still— family. We've got to let our relationships become more important than these material things or any other reasons for these family conflicts.

I had a learning experience in my own life of this kind years ago, and to resolve it I had to take the "low road" and choose to let it go! Sometimes you may want the material things, not because you are greedy but it may be for sentimental reasons related to the precious memories you have of your loved one. Even so, it is still not worth falling out about. Just let it go! Then trust God to resolve it in his own way and time.

You may not realize it right now, but you will need one another more than ever to get through this season of your lives together. So, I want to encourage you to forgive one another and walk in love.

This is so pleasing in the sight of God. It is also a good way to protect your own family circle, by choosing to forgive!

Does God feel the pain of all that we are going through and the tears we are pouring out through our grief? Absolutely yes! I am sure I have mentioned before that the bible says *"he can be touched with the feelings of our infirmities"* Did you know that the bible also says God puts our tears in a bottle? That's in Psalm 56:8. Wow! That's a powerful expression, I think, of how much He really cares. Here's the scripture I would give to Carmen all the time concerning her tears. It's Psalm 126:5-6 which says,

> **"They that sow in tears shall reap in joy. He that goeth forth and weepeth, bearing precious seed, shall doubtless come again with rejoicing, bringing his sheaves with him."**

Isn't it powerful that when Carmen was doing all that crying, especially for souls to be saved, that she was sowing precious seed? The New Living Translation makes this scripture even clearer to us when it says, *"Those who plant in tears will harvest with shouts of joy, they weep as they go to plant their seed, but they sing as they return with the harvest."* Wow! That is awesome! That puts another spin on crying and weeping, doesn't it!

God only knows how many souls have been harvested into the Kingdom through Carmen's ministry of tears. You will reap a harvest off of yours too! Remember: *"weeping may endure for a night but joy cometh in the morning"* (Psalm 30:5). It's morning time! So, let the singing and rejoicing begin!

CHAPTER 9

HEALER OF MY BROKEN HEART

"The Spirit of the Lord is upon me, because he hath anointed me to preach the gospel to the poor; he hath sent me to heal the brokenhearted, to preach deliverance to the captives, and recovering of sight to the blind, to set at liberty them that are bruised, to preach the acceptable year of the Lord."

Luke 4:18-19

"The Lord is close to the brokenhearted and saves those who are crushed in spirit."

Psalm 34:18 (NIV)

"A glad heart makes a cheerful countenance, but by sorrow of heart the spirit is broken."

Proverbs 15:13

When I began to think about what I would say to you in this chapter on the broken-hearted, I remembered the little nursery rhyme of Humpty Dumpty. It went like this: "Humpty Dumpty sat on a wall, Humpty Dumpty had a great fall. All the king's horses and all the king's men couldn't put Humpty together again."[11] Wow! What a devastating fall that must have been. No natural effort was able to put him back together again. What do you do when something has broken that seems to be beyond repair?

Most of the time, if you break something like fine china and you try to glue it back together, it will never be the same. It just doesn't look right. When you hold it up you can still see all the cracks in it. You will probably be tempted to just throw it into the trash. It seems worthless now that it's been broken. That's the way we handle external things when they break; we just throw them out with the trash! But what happens when the same experience happens on the inside of your life—called your heart? What do you do with a broken heart?

Talk about a broken heart, do I ever feel you in this moment in time, more than I can say. As hard as I may try to express how I felt when my beloved sister passed from this expression of life, I still find it hard to put into words. As I stood there looking at the casket and the physical house she once lived in, I was numb and overwhelmed with grief and sorrow. This was not the way I thought this story would end on this side of life. I was emotionally spent and truly needed some comfort, from the God of all comfort!

Although God will have people who love you do the nicest things for you to help heal your broken heart, sometimes you just can't seem to find a place of comfort. Don't feel guilty about feeling this way, because it's just all a part of the grieving process. However, I do want to admonish you by telling you that there is healing—real, lasting healing—for your broken heart. You just might not be looking for it in the right places.

Sometimes people try to find comfort in unhealthy relationships, in addictive and illegal drugs (which many people are dying from right now), or even in a bottle of alcoholic beverages. Some people are searching through the internet, or through other aspects of social media; in order to befriend perfect strangers for companionship and love.

There are so many other "temporary methods" of escape that people are using all over the world, to find comfort. They do this because they are looking for some relief from the pain of it all. They are often seeking to numb the pain. They are desperately searching for some way to forget the gravity of what has happened, only to find out that these temporary measures won't last. Every "artificial high" will end up bringing you down lower than you were before. Sooner or later it will all wear off, and you will still have to face the reality of the pain of a broken heart. Nothing will work until you choose to come to the one who can fix anything!

My Father Can Fix Anything

Some time ago I was working in a Christian bookstore and wanted to get a gift for my grandson, Joshua, for his birthday. I started browsing through the t-shirt section since I knew he liked those, and I ran across the perfect one. The writing on the shirt said "My Father can fix anything." The graphics on it were a nail, a hammer and a bloodstain, meant to represent the death of Jesus on the cross for our sins. I just loved it, and have never forgotten it to this day.

That's the message I want to get over to you in this trying season of your life—that your Father, God, can fix anything. The LORD said so Himself in Jeremiah 32:37,

> **"Behold, I am the LORD, the God of all flesh: is there anything too hard for me?"**

Jeremiah the Prophet says in the same chapter of the book of Jeremiah, vs. 17:

> **"Ah Lord God! Behold, thou hast made the heavens and the earth by thy great power and stretched out arm, and there is nothing too hard for thee."**

There are some tight places you get into in this life, and only God can bring your life back to a place of wholeness, as you look to Him. He's just waiting patiently to comfort you. How do I know that? It's because he reveals himself, in 2 Corinthians 1:3-4 (a scripture that I mentioned to you earlier), as the God of all comfort. This verse says:

> **"Blessed be God, even the Father of our Lord Jesus Christ, the Father of mercies, and the God of all comfort; who comforteth us in all our tribulation, that we may be able to comfort them which are in any trouble, by the comfort wherewith we ourselves are comforted of God."**

Human hands are certainly helpful in times like these, but nobody can comfort you quite like God can. The word "comfort" in the Greek is "paraklesis," which means *"to stand beside."* It means to encourage or to help someone in the time of trouble. God in his great love for us sent us a "helper" in the person of the Holy Spirit, who comes alongside of us to comfort us. Out of this ongoing comfort that He extends to us, we learn to extend that same comfort to others, just as this scripture said.

Receiving the Lord's Comfort

The Lord's comfort must be "received" first, before we can effectively extend it to others. What I mean by saying this is that there are several scriptures in the Bible that mention people who refused to be comforted. One example is when Jacob refused to be comforted over Joseph his son, when he thought he was dead. In Genesis 37:35, it says,

> **"His family all tried to comfort him but he refused to be comforted. No, he said, "I will go to my grave mourning for my son." (NIV)**

Have you "received" the Lord's comfort concerning your loved one? That's a question only you can answer. If not, I want to encourage you to let him comfort you right now. The Holy Spirit is waiting ever so patiently at this very moment to perform his ministry of comfort in you.

The Lord says something so comforting to us in I Thessalonians 4:13-18, concerning our loved ones who are now asleep in Jesus. It says,

> **"But I would not have you to be ignorant brethren, concerning them which are asleep, that ye sorrow not, even as others which have no hope. For if we believe that Jesus died and rose again, even so them also which sleep in Jesus will God bring with him. For this we say unto you by the word of the Lord, that we which are alive and remain unto the coming of the Lord shall not prevent them which are asleep.**

> **For the Lord himself shall descend from heaven with a shout, with the voice of the archangel, and with the trump of God: and the dead in Christ shall rise first:**

> Then we which are alive and remain shall be
> caught up together with them in the clouds,
> to meet the Lord in the air: and so shall we
> ever be with the Lord. Wherefore comfort
> one another with these words."

Did you hear what the apostle Paul said who wrote this letter to the Thessalonians? He said "comfort one another with these words."

I want to challenge you to read this powerful text in another translation so that you can get more of the depth of its meaning, like in the New Living Translation (NLT) or The Message Bible (MSG). You will really be blessed by it. In closing, I want to encourage you to receive the Lord's comfort by just saying out loud, "Lord, I 'receive' your comfort right now by faith concerning my loved one,

_____

(place the name of your loved one here).

Remember: it is by *faith*, not by *feeling*. Then the healing of your broken heart will begin. God will begin to impart life to your spirit and heal you in your broken places, in some absolutely amazing ways. He will begin to put you back together again far better than in that little nursery rhyme "Humpty Dumpty." You may not even realize when the healing begins, but it will be happening deep on the inside of your broken heart; because my Father—who is hopefully your Father—can fix anything!

CHAPTER 10

GROW IN GRACE

"For by grace are ye saved through faith, and that not of yourselves: it is the gift of God"

Ephesians 2:8

"But grow in grace, and in the knowledge of our Lord and Saviour, Jesus Christ. To him be glory both now and forever. Amen."

2 Peter 3:18

Most of you reading this book have heard of the old song called "Amazing Grace." It is one of the most well-beloved songs among believers in Jesus Christ, all over the world. I thought I understood the meaning of the grace of God until the passing of my beloved sister. It wasn't until I had begun to study the scriptures on this topic of grace (along with books that my pastor has written along these lines), that I saw another aspect of grace. I began to understand that this topic was more profound than I may have originally thought.

Although I can't go into all of the revelation that's been unfolding in my spirit (as I dig deeper in God's Word), I do want to share how the grace of God relates to this topic of grieving, in the passing of our loved ones.

Back in Old Testament times, the people of God lived under the law. Everything was about keeping rules and regulations, because Jesus Christ had not yet come in the flesh. The people had to bring animal sacrifices for their sins over and over again. Then the High Priest would go into the tabernacle (behind the veil in the Holy of Holies) once a year to make "atonement" (i.e. at-one-ment, or to be reconciled) for his own sins—and the sins of the people of God, called the Israelites.

This all took place under the Old Covenant that the people had with God, but now since Jesus Christ came and died for our sins (once and for all), we are no longer serving God under the *law* but rather under *grace* (Romans 6:14).

One of the definitions of grace is "unmerited favour." It is a gracious act of kindness that God bestowed upon us when he saved us from our sins, through the sacrificial death of Jesus Christ (Eph. 2:8,9). It expresses the heart attitude of God toward people whom He loves. It describes His willingness to be deeply involved with us. It causes Him to be moved with compassion toward us, and to supply His divine resources freely toward us from day to day. However, the other aspect of this awesome grace is seen as the "power" that is active within our hearts as believers, working within us and empowering us to do the will of God from our hearts, for His glory in the earth.

Grace for Grieving

At this point you might be wondering why this issue of grace is so important to us during the grieving process. It's because now that Christ has come, we can live our everyday lives *"by grace through faith,"* which makes supernatural *strength* available to us.

But the question is how do we tap into the "strength" we so desperately need in this season? There must be a *dependency* upon the grace of God to put us over in every situation. Our natural tendency is to seek to *depend* upon ourselves or others, when tragic or devastating things happen in our lives. We may start trying to think up ways to make it on our own, which is actually a work of the flesh. Self-effort apart from God is a sure defeat! Anything done in the flesh just won't last!

At other times, we may start trying to think of people we can call on, to help us out of these "crisis" situations. While it is true that we need people indeed, our greatest dependency must always be upon the Lord, above all else. He is always a very present help in times of trouble, in every season of our lives (Psa. 46:1).

Everything we are trying to do or get through must flow through receiving His amazing grace. We must now learn to see grace as "divine enablement," i.e. ability. It is the power and the desire to do His will from our hearts. We are to draw strength through our union with Him (I Cor. 6:17). It is something that flows from the realm of the Spirit. It's Spirit to spirit strength that flows out of our "union," i.e. oneness, with Him! This is so important, because through this means of grace we *draw* the necessary strength to get through what we've got to get through, without becoming depressed and discouraged in the process.

When a loved one has passed on you are going to need strength. Not our own human strength so much, but *supernatural strength* that can only come from God to go on without our loved ones, in this expression of life. You will need strength to go on with life even when you don't feel like it and don't want to. You must go on at some point, as I have encouraged you to do before.

God does allow us a period of grieving for a time, thankfully. However, there does come a time when God will compel you to go on from where you are and—live. Not just "exist," but live life to its fullest with love, joy and peace in your heart. It is the "abundant life" that Jesus died to give you and I (John 10:10).

You see, your emotions will try to control you and discourage you from going on. Your emotions (which can sometimes be like riding on a rollercoaster) are a part of your soul which is made up of your mind, will, and emotions. On those emotional days, you may even feel like you don't want to get out of bed, eat or socialize with family members or friends.

I remember only too well how I was at first when Carmen passed. I went back to my apartment and laid across my bed. I didn't feel like doing anything but grieving. I felt like I could have stayed in my bed for days without end. I would lay there for hours, playing soft music, and trying to get some relief from the daily sorrow that was filling my heart. I can't even put into words how bad I really felt. So many memories were flashing through my mind. So many questions, so much pain at having to face this new reality that could not be changed. No matter what I said or did, I knew it was over.

How do you access this grace that produces a supernatural strength you need for the journey? Grace is given in the time of "need" according to the scriptures. What better time than when you are grieving than to be able to access the grace of God?

We must remember that this grace is given to the humble (Jas. 4:6). So, when we resist the "pride" of trying to act like we still have it all together and just admit to the Lord that we need help, then we will receive more grace to help us overcome the next hurdle.

Actually, the grace of God is already living within us (Eph. 4:7). It's kind of like tap water. It's already in your house through the pipes, but it is not released until you turn the faucet on. In the same way, the grace of God is already there, if you have received the Lord Jesus Christ into your heart by faith; you just need to tap into it.

In the scriptures, one of the many ways that the Holy Spirit is referred to is as "the Spirit of Grace" (Hebrews 10:29). Therefore, since the Holy Spirit already lives within us, we already have the grace of God (2 Corinthians 12:8-9). However, there are seasons when we need "more" grace. That's why the scriptures say, when referring to grace, "more grace" (James 4:6), "great grace" (Acts 4:33) "abundant grace" (I Timothy 1:14), and so forth.

Sometimes you need *more* to get through the greater challenges, like when someone passes away. We also need what the apostle Paul calls, "The Word of His Grace" in Acts 20:32. I think of this like a word in season, that is referred to as "a Rhema word." It's a word that God quickens to you (by His Spirit) in your time of need. It's a word of His grace that is filled with the promises of God, that we can hold on to for times like these. It strengthens us when we get a "specific" word that is tailor-made for our situation. These types of words build you up where you may be torn down.

I just need you to know that you don't always have to be seeking out personal words from the prophetic gifts we have in the body of Christ, though some of them can be a real blessing. Prophecy is good and biblical, but you still need to know that you can hear from God too! He can give you a rhema word (a spoken word) that quickens in your spirit, to comfort and heal you in those broken places.

We have to keep drawing strength daily through our union with Him, as we seek to get through the process. You can even do that right now. Just raise your hands to the Lord for a moment and tell him,

> **Lord, I really need your help to get through this difficult time. I receive your grace for grieving right now in Jesus Name!**

Then, watch how he responds. You may be surprised at the way supernatural strength will come to lift you up from where you are, to where He wants you to be! It's absolutely amazing! I think that's why the song is called, "Amazing Grace."

Grace for Trusting

In times like these we may find that we cannot trace Him; therefore, we've just got to *trust* Him! God is so deep, so high, so wide, that sometimes you just can't trace Him. His ways and His thoughts are just higher than ours "just as the heavens are higher than the earth" (Isa. 55:9).

The scriptures describe to us (in so many wonderful ways) the awesomeness of the God we serve. His Word seeks to help us understand, what we in our *finite* minds (which have so many limitations) will never be totally able to understand or comprehend, about an in*finite* God who has no limitations. Even in light of how well we may think we know the eternal God, right now, there is still so much more to know. The truth is we will still be learning who this great and mighty God is that we serve—throughout eternity!

The bible uses other names for God to try to help us in our understanding of what God is like. It uses names like Jehovah-jireh, meaning "the Lord will provide," and yet we still do not understand the depth of his provision for us in Christ.

There is the name Jehovah-rapha, meaning "the Lord our healer," but even after much study of God's Word, we still don't fully understand the depth of the healing power of God—nor do we understand all aspects of healing and wholeness in Him. Then there is another name, Jehovah-shalom, meaning "He is our peace," and yet we do not fully comprehend this God of peace.

Isn't it amazing that there is peace *with* God (Rom. 5:1), and the peace *of* God (Phil. 4:7), which gives us peace within ourselves? Therefore, we are able to live in peace with our brothers and sisters in Christ (I Thess. 5:13b). That is absolutely powerful! We don't fully understand how God can give us His peace right in the midst of a traumatic situation—the kind of peace that has the power to keep us *stable,* through the grieving process. He is just a mighty awesome God.

He reveals himself in so many ways because he wants to be *known,* and he wants us to make *His name* known throughout the earth. Who can compare to Him? There is just none like Him! There will always be far more about our awesome God than we can ever imagine. That's why we should always be seeking to know Him more and more...as we go through the journey of life!

Unanswered Questions

It is also true, that even though we may have questions (about things that have happened in our lives upon the earth), some of them may never be answered in this expression of life. Though all these questions may seem so important to us on this side of life, I really don't think that they will be that important to us when we get on the other side—called heaven.

I do not think that we will get into the very presence of the Lord, behold how awesome He is, and say to Him,

> "Now Lord, I don't see why you let my loved one leave life in the earth realm with me so early. That was my grandma and grandpa, my father, my mother, my child, my sister, my brother or my best friend in all the world. How could you do such a thing or even allow it?"

You may have been saying all of these things while you were still here on earth, but from the heavenly perspective on the other side; would these things still be a major sticking point?

Do you really think that you will be saying things like that to the one who saved you from your sins *after* you are in His awesome presence? When you see Jesus face to face?

I really don't think so. No, I think you will be bowing down in worship, praising, and giving honor and thanksgiving, to the King of kings and the Lord of lords! You will be in such a celebration mode, that you even made it to heaven, and rejoicing to behold Jesus (the precious Lamb of God who taketh away the sins of the world)—face to face (I Cor. 13:12; I John 3:2; Rev. 22:4; John 1:29). Not to mention how you will be rejoicing to see your loved ones, who hopefully made it to heaven too. What an awesome reunion this will be! So, be willing to live with some *unanswered* questions.

> "Trust in the Lord with all thine heart. Lean not to your own understanding, in all your ways acknowledge him and he will direct your path."

Proverbs 3:5-6

I encourage you keep on fighting the good fight of faith, and keep on *trusting* Him even when you cannot *trace* Him!

CHAPTER 11

———————~———————

I KNOW THE PLANS

"I know the thoughts that I think toward you, thoughts of peace and not of evil to give you a hope and a future"

Jeremiah 29:11

"Many plans are in a man's heart, but the counsel of the LORD will stand."

Proverbs 19:21

I may have pointed this out earlier in another part of this book, but I think it bears repeating. Whenever Carmen would send you a greeting card for any occasion, it would most likely have this scripture in it, along with a smiley face. If it wasn't written out in longhand, you could be sure that you would see the text written on it—Jeremiah 29:11. She loved this verse and she wanted to make sure everyone she knew understood that God has a plan for each and every one of our lives. It was a word of encouragement on the importance of tapping into His plan.

She wanted us to keep our expectations for the future in God, in spite of whatever we might be going through or experiencing in this earth realm.

I decided to include this thought, in order to keep up this rhema legacy my covenant sister left to all of us. It's the constant reminder that we need to tap into, no matter what is going on in our lives. No matter the pain, trial, or tribulation, God still has a plan, so never give up! We need this to help keep us going. Why not try saying that out loud right now by faith, *"God has a good plan for my life."*

The plan may seem "altered" (from your perspective) now that your loved one is no longer here. Perhaps you thought you had it all mapped out as to what the two of you would be doing together, for years to come. You may have never imagined that they would be gone and you would still be here.

I know what you mean. I never imagined that I would still be here either and Carmen would be gone, especially since I was 10 years older than she was. I even remember telling my grandson, Joshua, one time that if anything ever happened to me, that he was to make sure that his auntie Carmen (as he always called her) was taken care of. That's how sure I must have felt that she would be here for many years to come.

However, I had to remember that those were "my plans," not necessarily God's plans. I had to be reminded that God has a *permissive* will and a *perfect* will. All things may not be framed in the context of His perfect will, but He still may choose to "allow" them. I guess I never thought about that when it came to her—that in God's permissive will He might let her transition from this life to the next, much earlier than I expected.

I think that must be why God often says to me,

"for my thoughts are higher than your thoughts and my ways higher than your ways"

Isaiah 55:8-9

Basically, it is another way of saying that we see in part, but God sees the fullness of the big picture of why He allows certain things to happen. So where does that leave us? Trusting Him even when we can't trace Him! That's just a little reminder!

Believe it or not, when I first started writing this book, a deep tragedy happened that brought much grief to so many families. There was a school shooting and 20 children were killed along with six adults in Connecticut. I began to cry as I thought of the heartbreak of those families who had lost their children. I thought of what it must have been like to arrive at the school and not be able to find your child, only to realize moments later that they were suddenly gone forever, from this expression of life. My heart was so filled with a deep compassion for those experiencing this level of grief, along with most of the rest of the world who were mourning with these families.

Since this tragedy, many devastating events have happened—far too numerous to mention. Some of them were more school shootings and even church shootings of nine people at one time. How tragic! The next question that comes to the mind of so many is the question "why" when things like this happen. Then, sometimes the reaction after that (for some who may be onlookers at this tragedy) is to blame God. However, I would not be so hasty right here to turn on the source of our help and only hope in this life, and the one to come.

Although I do not seek to get in a theological debate over this issue, I do want to say that, though this is a very deep and painful experience (that we might not completely understand), we can still keep our trust in the Lord—that is, if and only if we have come to really know who He is to some degree. He is a loving Father who cares for us all even when *unlovely* things may be happening all around us.

Actually, He already warned us about this life we live on earth, when He said to his disciples in John 16:33, 34:

> "I have told you these things, so that in Me you may have [perfect] peace. In the world you have tribulation and distress and suffering, but be courageous [be confident], be undaunted, be filled with joy]; I have overcome the world. [My conquest is accomplished, My victory abiding]" (AMP).

We as Christians must always keep in mind that we are living in a "fallen world," that began all the way back from the time of Adam and Eve (Genesis 3), and which is still being manipulated by the deceitfulness, craftiness, and subtleness of satan. Since we realize this, then our perspective of God must never be *tainted* by the evil that takes place in the context of this fallen world.

He is still the Almighty God and the Great I AM, even when we do not understand all the details of life from our perspective. You can see who He is—through the world He created, through His Word, and experience it out of your personal relationship with Him, through Jesus Christ—that He is a mighty awesome God! Bad things happening does not take anything away from who He is, or from His goodness; He is still GOD. Somebody just ought to say "amen" right here! Not only that, but He is still God all by Himself and nothing that happens will ever change that!

Many of the truths needed to come to know God in a more intimate way, can be found in great detail throughout the scriptures in times like these. I hope you will spend much time between the pages of the Holy Bible and come to know in a greater way, the King of kings and the Lord of lords.

You will be refreshed, renewed and revived to continue on the journey of life, understanding that God still has an awesome plan for your life.

I know you may not be able to trace him as you face circumstances like this, but can you still trust him? Remember, the bible says:

> **"Trust in the Lord with all your heart; and lean not unto thine own understanding. In all thy ways acknowledge him, and he shall direct thy paths."**
>
> **Proverbs 3:5-6**

Believe it or not, even in the midst of all this— God still has a good plan for your life! His thoughts of you are still of peace and not of evil, to give you a hope and a future! You are always on His mind!

CHAPTER 12

DON'T MISS THE SHIFT

"Enter into his gates with thanksgiving, and into his courts with praise: be thankful unto him, and bless his name. For the LORD is good; his mercy is everlasting; and his truth endureth to all generations"

Psalm 100: 4-5

"To appoint unto them that mourn in Zion, to give them beauty for ashes, the oil of joy for mourning, the garment of praise for the spirit of heaviness; that they may be called trees of righteousness, the planting of the LORD, that he might be glorified."

Isaiah 61:3

Sometimes when you have been grieving for a while (if you let it last too long), you may increase your potential to fall into a spirit of self-pity. You may start to feel sorry for yourself, and begin to seek out pity from others if you are not careful. This can even lead to depression and deep discouragement, if allowed to linger over your life. God does not want us to feel sorry for ourselves, because it turns all of our thoughts and attention upon ourselves. It leaves out the feelings of others and what they may be experiencing as well. It causes us to shut others out and make everything about ourselves rather than about God.

How do you avoid feeling sorry for yourself, when something so tragic has happened to you?

You are going to have to shake yourself out of that frame of mind, and rise up and take authority over that demonic spirit, which did *not* come from God. You are going to have to choose to receive the grace of God to make a shift from *grieving* to *gratitude,* according to the Word of God.

The book of Psalms would be a good place to begin to declare a spirit of thanksgiving over your life. We are instructed in the Word of God to give thanks unto the Lord for He is good and His mercy endures forever (Ps. 107:1). This is just one of many scriptures to help you get yourself stirred up in the Holy Spirit, for this yoke to be destroyed and this burden to be removed out of your life. To help you get started, I have listed some scriptures for you to declare out loud over your atmosphere. You can do this right there in your home right now, or wherever you are. God is waiting to hear from you right in the midst of your pain. He has not abandoned you.

He's waiting to comfort you as you turn to Him and seek His face in praise and worship. He will touch you in that secret place like nobody else can, and make you whole. So, why not lift up your voice and release your praise, in honor of the mighty God we serve.

So many of the breakthroughs that we seek, happen when we release a spirit of thanksgiving out of our mouths, during a time like what you are experiencing right now, in the grieving process. Thanksgiving is the pathway to worship according to Psalm 100, and once we enter into the realm of worship, anything can happen! Sometimes it's hard to get started because of the spirit of heaviness we feel in moments like this, but you can breakthrough it, by putting on the garment of praise for the spirit of heaviness (Isaiah 61:3).

So, here are a few verses to help jumpstart you, in renewing your mind to the power of thanksgiving and praise:

Note: Just read them out loud over and over again if you need to, until you sense a breakthrough coming up out of your spirit! Agree with God's Word and not how you feel.

- This is the day which the LORD hath made; we will rejoice and be glad in it. Psalms 118:24
- Bless the Lord oh my soul and all that is within me, bless his holy name. Psalms 103:1
- O give thanks unto the LORD; call upon his name: make known his deeds among the people Psalms 105:1
- O give thanks unto the LORD, for he is good: for his mercy endureth forever. Psalms 107:1
- Thou art my God, and I will praise thee; thou art my God, and I will exalt thee – Psalms 118:28
- Oh that men would praise the LORD for his goodness, and for his wonderful works to the children of men. And let them sacrifice the sacrifices of thanksgiving, and declare his works to the children of men! Psalms 107:21, 22.
- From the rising of the sun unto the going down of the same the LORD'S name is to be praised – Psalms 113:3
- I will offer unto thee the sacrifice of thanksgiving, and will call upon the name of the LORD – Psalms 116:17

Most of the time, giving thanks in the midst of a trial (whether it is someone's passing, or some other type of painful crisis) is—sacrificial. What makes it sacrificial is that emotionally (in our soulish realm) we don't feel like doing it, but as a believer and a doer of the Word of God, we do it by grace through faith; as I mentioned earlier.

The result of our obedience is a breakthrough, that only God can release to us in the midst of our praise and worship.

We need to experience the breaking of the oppression of a heavy spirit and the spirit of self-pity, "hovering" over our lives. The Word of God declared out of our mouth has the power to do just that! It is the power of the spoken word that can break these chains of defeat!

These demonic spirits make us want to shut down. Some people even lose their minds from all the stress and pressure of these devastating experiences of death. Because of this I am learning to make it a habit of "affirming" my faith out loud, concerning my state of mind. Especially during major warfare attacks that the enemy wages on the mind, when he sees you in a state of weakness. I confess that: *"I will never go crazy, I will always be in my right mind.* Then I go on to say, *"That's because I have the mind of Christ"* (I Cor. 2:16). Sometimes, it can get just that serious! When you are going through this type of battle for your mind, it's good to also have other strong believers to join you in the fight.

Coming Out of Isolation

The truth is that, there are times when some believers may get in such bad shape that they lose their desire to even want to fellowship with the saints. That may be because they are in so much pain, and therefore choose to live their lives in *a state of isolation;* which is sometimes referred to as being in a "backslidden" state. Is that you?

Even worse than that, some have entertained thoughts of suicide when feeling overcome by grief. This can also be a by-product of living your life in isolation.

Thoughts come to you that no one cares, or no one knows how you feel. It is a feeling of hopelessness, and there seems to be no way out. This is absolutely not true! These are lies from the enemy that you must take authority over, in Jesus' name!

Thoughts and imaginations of this kind must be pulled down according to 2 Corinthians 10:4-5. These suicidal thoughts may come, but this does not mean that they came from—God! Though we may feel really bad on the inside we must not allow this to happen. Why? God is the giver of all life according to the scriptures. So, that being true; do we really have the right to take the life that He created, and gave to us as a gift?

I know that this is a bit of a controversial subject, but I still feel that the truth must be spoken in love. The life God gave to you and me is *precious* and *valuable*. You are very important in His sight whether you are saved or not! Everyone that God created is valuable! You are also a valuable member of the body of Christ, if you are—in Christ. Everybody is important and everybody is necessary to the life of the body of Christ. We need you!

When we were saved, we became members of Christ, and members of a spiritual family called the body of Christ. Our being together is a vital life-giving "covenant connection" that must be maintained according to Hebrews 10:25. That's where we are instructed not to forsake the assembly of the saints as the manner of some is. Thanking and praising God together with other believers in Jesus Christ, will give you one of the greatest breakthroughs you can ever imagine. It encourages you to give thanks also when you see other believers wrapped up in thanksgiving and praise, especially when you know that they have their challenges too.

In this church setting you can also receive prayer and encouragement from being in the midst of other believers as well. You must remember you are not alone. Your brothers and sisters in Christ are going through serious challenges too in one way or another. It may not be the exact same experience as yours, but "pain is pain" when it comes right down to it. In I Peter 5:9, in the Amplified version, it says this about the sufferings of our brothers and sisters in the context of the body of Christ:

> Be sober [well balanced and self-disciplined], be alert and cautious at all times. That enemy of yours, the devil, prowls around like a roaring lion [fiercely hungry] seeking someone to devour. But resist him, be firm in your faith [against his attack—rooted, established, immovable], knowing that the same experiences of suffering are being experienced by your brothers and sisters throughout the world. [You do not suffer alone].

In the New Living Translation, this same verse reads this way:

> "Stay alert! Watch out for your great enemy, the devil. He prowls around like a roaring lion, looking for someone to devour. Stand firm against him, and be strong in your faith. "Remember that your Christian brothers and sisters all over the world are going through the same kind of suffering you are."
>
> I Peter 5:8-9 (NLT)

We are told to resist our enemy by faith, and it is even more effective when we do it together as a community of faith.

Even if you look around the sanctuary and all the saints seem to be smiling and rejoicing in the Lord, don't let that make you think that they aren't going through anything. They are just trusting God to see them through, just like you. All believers in Jesus Christ receive opposition from the devil, so you are not alone.

Therefore, I want to encourage you to go to your church home and praise God with your spiritual family that God has placed you in, and praise God together with them. If you do not have a church home, I encourage you to begin visiting somewhere that God will lead you to by His Spirit. Please do not just sit at home by yourself grieving alone, day after day.

That said, I do want you to make sure that you find your way to a good bible-believing church, that preaches the "full gospel" of Jesus Christ. By that I mean a church that believes in the death, burial and resurrection of Jesus Christ, His shed blood for our sins and the virgin birth, and that they celebrate Jesus as— Savior and Lord.

When you arrive at church I want you to believe God, together with your other hurting brothers and sisters, that He is bringing *all* of you out together because we, as the body of Christ, are—family! The bible says, *"God places the lonely in families; he sets the prisoners free and gives them joy "*(Psalms 68:6, NLT). Yes, we are family and family is important!

CHAPTER 13

A FRIEND FOR THE JOURNEY

"Greater love has no one than this, that someone lay down his life for his friends."

John 15:13

"Henceforth I call you not servants; for the servant knoweth not what his lord doeth: but I have called you friends; for all things that I have heard of my Father I have made known unto you"

John 15:15

"A man who has friends must himself be friendly, But there is a friend who sticks closer than a brother."

Proverbs 18:24 (NKJV)

You may remember me saying that when my friend Carmen passed (from this expression of life to the life hereafter in heaven), I would find myself feeling like I just lost my best friend in all the earth. Now that I had come to a deeper understanding of what friendship was all about through our covenant relationship, I wondered what I would do without her. I questioned in my mind if I would ever have another friend like her in my life. I began to think that friendships like this might be somewhat rare, because they require such a deep level of commitment on the part of both people. So, I guess you can see why I was really concerned about this.

That's when I began to think about a song I had heard some time ago. It was called "I Am a Friend of God." I began to sing it and reflect on its meaning. Then later I was reminded of a passage of scripture in the bible that talked about God being our friend (John 15:15). You can see this scripture at the beginning of this chapter.

As I began to study this scripture and gain insights into the meaning of it, I realized what God was trying to say to me. He was going to take me back to the story of Adam and Eve, and the fall of mankind, in order to broaden my understanding of friendship from His perspective. He reminded me that through this first man and woman upon the earth, sin and death had entered and passed upon all mankind. Therefore, the whole world had now been made "enemies" of God.

Then God did something so wonderful. He took action on our behalf by sending his only Son, Jesus, to save us from our sins, taking us off of that old cycle of sin and death, and making us alive in Christ Jesus. Not only did He do that (if that was not awesome enough), but in acting toward us in that low estate, He had made us His friends!

Now, instead of being His enemies we are on friendly terms with the God of the whole universe through Jesus Christ. It just does not get any better than that, does it? That's the good news of the gospel of Jesus Christ! It's called reconciliation. Our relationship with God has been "restored" through Jesus Christ! It has been put back together again.

Here is how the scriptures unfold this truth in Romans 5:8-17, from The Message Bible:

"But God put his love on the line for us by offering his Son in sacrificial death while we were of no use whatever to him. Now that we are set right with God by means of this sacrificial death, the consummate blood sacrifice, there is no longer a question of being at odds with God in any way.

If, when we were at our worst, we were put on friendly terms with God by the sacrificial death of his Son, now that we're at our best, just think of how our lives will expand and deepen by means of his resurrection life!

Now that we have actually received this amazing friendship with God, we are no longer content to simply say it in plodding prose. We sing and shout our praises to God through Jesus, the Messiah!

You know the story of how Adam landed us in the dilemma we're in—first sin, then death, and no one exempt from either sin or death.

That sin disturbed relations with God in everything and everyone, but the extent of the disturbance was not clear until God spelled it out in detail to Moses. So death, this huge abyss separating us from God, dominated the landscape from Adam to Moses.

Even those who didn't sin precisely as Adam did by disobeying a specific command of God still have to experience this termination of life, this separation from God. But Adam who got us into this, also points ahead to the One who will get us out of it.

Yet the rescuing gift is not exactly parallel to the death dealing sin. If one man's sin put crowds of people at the dead-end abyss of separation from God, just think what God's gift poured through one man, Jesus Christ will do!

There's no comparison between that death-dealing sin and this generous life-giving gift."

I had to type all of these verses out, because I realized that I just couldn't say it any better than that! God did all of this while we were still in our sins (Romans 5:8). We were separated, i.e., alienated, isolated, estranged, distant, from the presence of God because of sin, but God dealt with the sin problem by sending Jesus as the Savior of the World. He dealt with that which made us His "enemies" and in turn made us His "friends!" That's amazing!

Now, I feel some better about not having my precious friend with me in the earth realm. Will I miss her? Yes, every single day more than I can say (for now), until we meet again in the next expression of life called heaven!

However, I already have the ultimate friend in this life and in the one to come. That's because I am a friend of God's, through my Lord and Savior Jesus Christ! Yes, He is my friend for the journey!

All of the amazing characteristics I have told you about that were in Carmen can all be found in Him! He is just that kind of friend. She was just "modeling" the nature and characteristics of her Lord and Savior, Jesus Christ!

She was beholding as in a mirror the glory of the Lord and being changed into that same image (2 Cor. 3:18). It was the image of Christ manifesting itself in and through her. Guess what? He was her friend for the journey! That's why those of us who knew her experienced that fruit of love, joy, peace, longsuffering, gentleness, and so forth, from Galatians 5:22-23, which are the nine fruit that the Spirit produces in us. That's how she learned how to be such a great friend to me!

She was modeling the image she was beholding, in the Word of God! She was being changed into the same image by beholding the glory of the Lord in the face of Jesus Christ! That's powerful!

Open to New Friends?

Will I still need earthly friends? The answer is absolutely yes! Actually, I already have some wonderful covenant sisters at the Mount, who are a blessing in my life! I am also confident that the Lord will raise up other new ones, to continue to walk with me through the rest of the journey. Will they ever be able to take Carmen's place? No, because we are all uniquely created— according to God's divine design as individuals. Therefore, no one can ever be who we are.

There was only one Carmen D. Murray, although I am sure that some of her character qualities and sense of humor will show up in some of them in one way or another, and that will be a good thing!

Yes, I am sure that some of my new friends to come will fit like pieces snapped together in a puzzle. In His divine wisdom, I am certain that He has already shaped us to fit together (for what He knows that we both need) to continue the journey of life. We will come together, so we can effectively fulfill our assignment in the earth for His glory.

He will cause our paths to cross at just the right moment in time, for sure! I can only hope that I will have taken the principles that I learned from my precious friend, so that I can be that kind of friend to them as well!

Now that I have sought to answer some of the questions you may have had about a friend for the journey from this chapter, I want to ask you a very important question along these same lines.

Are You a Friend of God's?

I cannot help but ask you this question knowing that I have the best friend of all times. Whenever you have a really good friend in this natural realm, you want others to meet them because they are so special and precious to you. When you introduce your best friend to others, you may say something like this:

> "I would like to introduce you to my very best friend:"

_____

(write your friend's name here).

Sometimes you even begin to elaborate on the type of friendship you have with them. You may go on to say:

> "This is my bosom buddy. We have been together for 25 years. We are inseparable! She has always been there for me."

Then you will probably go on and on to describe how precious they are to you, and how you first met.

If that's true, naturally speaking, when you have a best (earthly) friend, how much more should this be true when we have a best friend in God through our Lord and Savior, Jesus Christ. We should not be selfish, but want others to meet him as well, right?

My Personal Testimony

Since I do not want to take for granted that you already know Him, I want to take a moment to introduce you to Him. Let me start off by saying that I met Him for the first time when I was about five years old. He has been my constant companion for life since that wonderful day. He was always there, but I wasn't introduced to Him until then. My mother used to always take me to church with her from an infant, but I still didn't know Him.

Then one day while I was in church with my mother, I heard the preacher give an invitation to come forward and receive Jesus as the Lord of my life. I don't think I really understood all of this at the time, but I felt something in my heart compelling me to come forward. So, I got up and walked down that aisle and gave my heart to the Lord. I knew something had happened in my life on the inside, but I had no idea of the impact this decision would have on my life for years to come.

After that experience with God, as I continued to grow up my parents would have family devotions in our household every week and expose me to the Word of God, which changed my life for the better—forever. I have had some ups and downs, some high days and some very low days too. However, in the midst of it all, I can truly say that He has always been by my side to give me courage and consolation, all through the journey of life. I learned over the years that He was a friend that sticks closer than a brother.

He said that He would never leave us or forsake us, and I have always found this to be true. All of our natural friends will have to leave us one day, but the good news is that (if we are saved and they were too), we can count on seeing them again. However, the friendship we have in Jesus is so unique in that He won't leave us in this life or in the one to come. We are inseparable!!! You see, what I did not know in my very young years, I know now.

I now understand that many years ago (when I made Jesus my choice by His grace), I had just become—a friend of God's!

I now had a friend for the journey throughout eternity! If you don't know this friend I am talking about, you can make that same choice to receive Him, just like I did many years ago. Just pray this prayer for salvation sincerely from your heart out loud, then you will become a friend of God's too!

PRAYER FOR SALVATION
(Please pray this prayer out loud)

Dear Heavenly Father,

"I come to you now, in the name of the Lord, Jesus Christ, recognizing my need of your great salvation. I repent of my sin of unbelief and renounce all rebellion and ungodliness. I believe that Jesus Christ died for my sins. I believe that He was buried, and that He arose again from the dead.

I, moreover, believe that He is enthroned at the right hand of the Majesty on high as King of kings and Lord of lords right now. According to God's Holy Word, I confess with my mouth that Jesus is Lord.

I own Him now as my King and I call upon Him to save me as He has promised. Now, by faith I give you thanks, dear Jesus, for saving me and making me your child. Amen."[12]

I am so excited for you, and the decision you just made to accept Jesus Christ as your personal Lord and Savior! Now I want to encourage you to take your next step by joining a good church home that teaches the truth about who Jesus is, and the blood He shed for you at the cross for your sins. You will need some place to "grow up" and be able to fellowship with the family of God.

Cut Flowers Don't Grow

My Pastor has many favorite sayings that he uses when he is preaching, and one of them is *"cut flowers don't grow!"* What he is saying is when you buy flowers at the flower shop, as beautiful as they are, you already know that they have been cut off from their life source.

You then take them home and put them in a vase with water. The next thing you may do, is put the preservative packet inside of the vase with water. You have now done everything you can to preserve them for as long as possible. However, at some point, sooner than later, they will die. Why? Because they have been disconnected from the source of life that they originated from.

That's kind of what it is like to not have a good church home. You cannot grow up properly without being connected to your brothers and sisters in Christ. Since we are the body of Christ, we must be connected just like the human body is. The body of Christ was created to be vitally connected, and working together in covenant love.

When you were saved, you entered into the door of a redeemed community, of born again believers in Jesus Christ (John 10:9-11). You will need to meet your new brothers and sisters in Christ, since you are now a part of the greatest family on earth called the body of Christ. You must learn to live together with them and serve out your purpose in the earth together as one, for His glory!

Also, you need never doubt from this point on that you are truly an "authentic" child of God, and a vital member of the body of Christ. Not because I said so, but because the bible says,

"The Spirit himself bears witness with our spirit that we are the children of God."
Rom. 8:16

That is simply amazing, isn't it!

I want to encourage you to say it for yourself. Say, *"I am a child of the one true and living God,"* then rejoice in the God of your Salvation! It is a new day in your life. Be sure to record this special day of your "new birth" in Christ, and tell it to generations yet to come of how God changed your life! You can even record it right here if you like.

Born Again on: (Day) _____ (Month) _____

(Date)_____ (Year)_____

May the Lord bless you and keep you!

> **"Jesus replied, 'Very truly I tell you, no one can see the kingdom of God unless they are born again.'**
>
> **John 3:3 (NIV)**

> **"Except a man be born of water and of the Spirit, he cannot enter into the kingdom of God."**
>
> **John 3:5**

There are many other important steps you must be willing to take from here, so that you can walk in the fullness of all that God has for you. That's why I want to encourage you to go into the waters of baptism as soon as possible.

Please don't delay in making your "identification" with Jesus Christ in His death, burial and resurrection, so you can begin to walk in the newness of this amazing life that you have just entered into! It's a new identity and a new life in Christ, and there are many other amazing experiences awaiting you as you learn what it really means to be—in Christ! Read Romans 6:4.

CHAPTER 14

JOURNALING THE JOURNEY

"Now Jacob's well was there. Jesus therefore, being wearied with his journey, sat thus on the well...

John 4:6

"In journeyings often, in perils of waters, in perils of robbers, in perils by my own countrymen, in perils by the heathen, in perils in the city, in perils in the wilderness, in perils in the sea, in perils among false brethren; in weariness and painfulness..., in hunger and thirst, in fastings often, in cold and nakedness.

2 Corinthians 11:26-27

I may have said earlier that life is a *journey,* and indeed it is. Through my own personal experience, I have discovered how important it is to *journal the journey* of our life in Christ, which we are traveling on from glory to glory.

I have always loved to write from a very young age. What I never knew, however, until years later (as I developed in my relationship and fellowship with God), is what it meant to be able to hear from God and write down what he said to me. After I got this revelation, I used to journal all the time. I would go to the bible bookstore and buy journals quite often. I would fill them up with notes and then need to get another one. It seems like I have hundreds of them now.

Over time, I gradually drifted away from these divinely inspired writings. However, when my covenant sister Carmen passed, a precious saint of God had the sensitivity to the Holy Spirit to understand that I would need to journal, in this critical season in my life. So, I was given the gift of a large new beautiful journal to use in my "sacred space" with God. It is a gift that I will treasure always.

This gift prompted me to begin journaling once again. Now I have pages and pages of many notes from the journey, as I continue to spend precious time with God. It has been absolutely amazing to read back over them from time to time, reflecting on the things God has said to me since Carmen's passing! He is such an awesome God!

One day, prior to Carmen's transition, my pastor asked me to attend a workshop, along with a few other members of my church. The conference was out of town (though it was not too far away). However, I found myself being so reluctant to go because of the physical condition of my friend at this point in her life. I was in such a dilemma at first because it seemed, from a natural perspective, to be the worst time to be leaving on a trip. Fear tried to grip me through imaginations about the possibility of her passing while I was away. I felt a deep need to be at her bedside 24/7 to help her in any way I could.

Knowing my pastor as I have for so many, many years, I knew he would never ask me to do something like this in the midst of a crisis—unless he had heard from God. After all, he and my Co-Pastor loved her so deeply as well, and I knew they both would find it hard to be away during this time. So, I mentioned it to Carmen and she insisted that I go, even though I kept expressing my reluctance to her.

She assured me that she would be okay until I came back, so I decided to go. Thank God that when I returned she was still hanging on by the grace of God. That was His faithfulness showing up once again, and granting our request.

I will never be able to thank God enough for leading my pastor to ask me to attend that life-changing seminar. I now know that it was entirely in the plan of God for my life to "stabilize" me for what I was about to experience, on the next part of the journey. Not even knowing exactly what this seminar was about, I sensed the peace of God to go, and so I went.

When I arrived, and walked into the room, I discovered that the topic was—How to Hear from God. It was being conducted by a man named Mark Virkler. He and his wife wrote a book together called *4 Keys to Hearing God's Voice*. I must say that I had never heard teaching from this type of perspective on how to hear from God, and was I ever going to need it, once my beloved friend passed—far more than I could have even imagined at that moment in time.

Not very long after my return home from the trip, my precious sister in Christ made her transition to her eternal home, to be with the Lord. It was devastating to say the least. We had of course previously fasted, prayed, supported, and undergirded her in every way possible, trusting that she would be kept in this expression of life.

Only the Lord knows the depths we went to, believing that she would make it through this ultimate challenge. So many unanswered questions arose in my heart and, I am sure, also in the hearts of her mother, her sister, our church family and multitudes of friends of this family as well.

She was just that type of woman of God that you could never imagine her not being here anymore, in this realm of life. It was just inconceivable in our minds. What would life be like now for those of us left here with her presence being gone from among us? It seemed that everything had changed. How would we adjust? Why did it turn out like this? So many questions indeed!

These and so many other types of questions began to rapidly fill up my mind. However, because I had just attended the seminar (and it was still so fresh within me), I was clear on what I had to do, in spite of how I felt in my soulish realm, i.e., emotions. I must clear space to spend time hearing from God.

I went to my desk (the place where I spend quiet time with him and knuckled down in order to quiet my soul, so I could hear his voice deep within me. That's what it says in Psalms 131:2:

"I have calmed and quieted my soul, like a weaned child with its mother; like a weaned child is my soul within me" (ESV).

After settling down, I followed the principles I had learned at the seminar, so that I would be able to hear Him more clearly.

Normally, I tend not to share personal things like this from my intimate times with God, but I feel impressed to share a portion of it with you in this book. Hopefully, it will be a reminder to you that all of us who are born again believers in Jesus Christ can hear from God. The ability to hear God flows out of your intimacy with Him, and your willingness to set aside some quiet time with Him. Just like you do when you have a really good friend, you want to spend time with them.

Nobody is twisting your arm to be with them. It's the desire of your heart to be in their presence. God wants to speak to his people, he wants to encourage, and strengthen us through the storms of life, and impart fresh revelation and fresh direction for the journey.

He wants us to know how much He cares and that He is with us in every storm, for we are never alone when He is with us. Jesus even said this of Himself when He was going to be abandoned by his disciples. He prophetically spoke these words,

> **"Behold, the hour cometh, yea, is now come, that ye shall be scattered every man to his own, and shall leave me alone: and yet I am not alone, because the Father is with me."**
>
> **John 16:32**

Jesus knew what it was like to feel alone without the support of his disciples, but yet He said He was not alone because his Father was with Him. So, anytime that the presence of the Lord is there, we are never alone either. In fact, that is where our joy is; it's in His presence. *"In his presence is fullness of joy"* (Psalms 16:11). He is our constant companion and He is waiting to guide us through the journey of life, if we are willing to take time to *listen* for His voice.

A Note from my Journal

In this particular note from my journal, I was asking God a question, as Mark Virkler taught us in the seminar, in order to better hear from God. He reminded us that God wants to hear our questions. So, the question that I presented to the Lord was, *Lord, what about groaning's?*

I asked this question of the Lord today, because of a study I was doing at the time in Romans the 8th chapter about the *sufferings* and the *glory* spoken of in this text. I started this study because I needed to be comforted concerning my sister beloved. I was reminded that the scriptures had said in Romans 15:4:

> "For whatsoever things were written aforetime were written for our learning, that we through patience and comfort of the scriptures might have hope."

Without a doubt, I knew that I was going to need hope in this crisis season of my life. As I studied His Word, I felt the Lord speaking to me about Carmen and her sufferings for Christ. This was His reply that I sensed flowing out of my born-again spirit:

> Carmen's physical pain represented a spiritual pain and groaning in the Spirit. She was "groaning for the glory." She was awaiting the manifestation of the sons of God. She was travailing in the Spirit realm for the church—the body of Christ, specifically for the saints of Mt. Zion that the purpose of God for the church in the earth to be revealed, so that people who do not know the Lord would see Him through the manifestation of the sons of God.
>
> Groaning's are so painful. It's pain with a purpose, pain with sorrow. It's a necessary pain that brings forth the purpose of God. Not everyone is willing to pay the price of travailing for change.

It cost, it's a sacrifice. It brings forth my glory in the earth. I'm looking for a glorious church, a church without spot or wrinkles. A holy church set apart and sanctified for my use. Groaning is deep.

Groaning's go the core of the issue, the very heart of the matter. They are gut level groaning's, unearthing all that hinders the manifestation of the true sons of God. It addresses those things that are holding back and obstructing my purpose in the earth. It reveals, it exposes those things. It removes the barriers.

The Holy Spirit helps you to groan. He groans through you as you yield yourself to Him. You must long for, look for, expect and pay the price to see the manifestation of the true sons of God. You must hunger for it and long for it with all your heart. You must press in, press in. Press in deeper. Look, long for, search in the Spirit to see my purpose established in the earth—I'm waiting.

You see, I was so overwhelmed by the physical pain that she was in, and how she could not seem to get any real relief. Even when the doctors would increase the dosages, she still couldn't get a sustainable breakthrough. It is so painful to watch someone you love be in intense physical pain and you can't help them, even with your best efforts. So, you can imagine how much I appreciated the Lord sharing these insights with me, to help me see a different perspective of the pain. I am sure that all Carmen was experiencing in her sufferings, were not only for this reason I stated in my journal.

However, I thank God that he chose to share with me some insights from His perspective. Perhaps, in the days ahead, He will choose to reveal even more than this, as I seek to hear from Him through the awesome power of effectual fervent prayer (James 5:16b).

We all have different pain thresholds, so some of us can endure perhaps more pain than others. But I was thinking about what helps you endure this kind of intense pain that Carmen went through. One of the ways I think she got through it as well as she did, was because of her *intimacy* with God through prayer. Not only that, but it was also the time she invested in His Word that gave her supernatural strength to endure. She had stored up ammunition in her heart against the enemy of her soul! I think she felt like Job when he said:

> **"Neither have I gone back from the commandments of his lips; I have esteemed the words of his mouth more than my necessary food."**
>
> **Job 23:12**

When she was hospitalized, Carmen would read the Word from her hard copy bible as often as she could. If she wasn't up to it, she would take her earphones and her device with the bible recorded on it, and listen to it being read by someone else. She wanted to keep the *truth* going in her ears and into her heart on a consistent basis. She was drawing strength for the battle through her communion with Him!

Here are a few scriptures on prayer that you can meditate upon, so you can be reminded of just how important it is to spend time hearing from God in prayer.

1 John 5:14; 1 Chron. 16:11; 2 Chron. 6:21; 2 Chron. 7:14; Eph. 1:18; Eph. 6:18; Jer. 29:12; Mark 11:24; Matt. 5:44; Matt. 26:41.

I especially want you to read the 17th chapter of John, which is known as Jesus' High Priestly Prayer, that He prayed to the Father. It is so powerful! He understood and modeled the power of prayer, and we should feel compelled to follow His lead too!

Since we have been talking about prayer and intimacy with God through prayer in this chapter on journaling the journey, I thought I would share something else with you in closing. One time, years ago, I told Carmen that I wanted to do a bookmark on prayer. Since I knew what a powerful intercessor she was, I wanted to hear what God would release through her on this topic.

I asked her to do an acronym for the word— prayer. She did it too, but she wouldn't let me put her name on it, as the author of it. That was how humble she was, so nobody ever knew she wrote it and she wouldn't let me tell anyone either. However, now I think I have a release to write it out to be a blessing to you.

She wanted to make our understanding of prayer more simplistic. So, we will call it, "THE SIMPLICITY OF PRAYER" in her honor! Here is the layout she did, in her own words:

THE SIMPLICITY OF PRAYER

P   **Powerful** tool used to communicate with the heavenly Father and co-labor with Him in the earth (Ephesians 1:17-19)

R   **Remain** humble in His presence and receive his amazing grace (I Peter 5:5-7)

A   **Acknowledge** Him in all your ways and He shall direct your path (Proverbs 3:5-6)

Y   **Yield** to the work of the Holy Spirit that He may minister to you in those secret places (Psalm 51)

E   **Expect** God to do exceedingly, abundantly above all you can ask or think, according to the power that is at work in you (Ephesians 3:20)

R   **Remember**, absolutely that God loves you and that nothing will separate you from His love!!! (Romans 8:35-38)

───────────〜〜───────────

On the other side of the bookmark she wrote:

2 Chronicles 7:14,

> **"If my people, which are called by my name, shall humble themselves, and pray, and seek my face, and turn from their wicked ways; then will I hear from heaven, and will forgive their sin, and will heal their land.**

CHAPTER 15

LEAVING A LEGACY

"Peace I leave with you, my peace I give unto you: Let not your heart be trouble neither let it be afraid."

John 14:27

"Now also when I am old and grayheaded, O God, forsake me not; until I have shewed thy strength unto this generation, and thy power to everyone that is to come."

Psalm 71:18

When you hear the term legacy, your first thoughts may be of getting older or about facing the reality of death, but actually it is all about life, loving and sharing your life with others. We need to think of it more as a "gift" we give, that interconnects one generation to another. Legacy has to do with something that is of significance or value being handed down from generation to generation. It means that you feel some since of responsibility to be a blessing to those who are coming after you.

Whether we see it this way or not right now, it is also an act of "gratitude" on your part to leave a legacy. When you take the time to reflect on all that God has given to you, you then realize that you are being given the opportunity to impact others through those gifts, talents, and abilities.

Then you will feel compelled to work through "procrastination" that most often holds us back from leaving something here in the earth.

The focus of leaving a legacy should not be about meditating on the end of your life, so much. It's more about realizing that you have been blessed to be a blessing in the earth (Gen. 12:1-3) as the blessed seed of Abraham. From a biblical perspective, we should all be looking forward to having something we can impart to the coming generations, to help them get through the journey of life.

These coming generations are really going to have something to face, when we are gone from this expression of life, since they will be left here in a "fallen world"—right in the midst of a crooked and perverse generation (Phil. 2:15).

They are going to need all the revelation we have received over the years, and all the help they can get, for sure! They will need our books, songs, prayers, and faith stories, about how we made it through the journey of life. Besides all this, Jesus left us a legacy when He left this earth realm, so how can we think of doing anything less!

When Jesus left this earth realm, He left us an awesome legacy of—peace. It's found in the book of John 14:27, where he says:

> **"Peace I leave with you, my peace I give unto you: . . . Let not your heart be troubled, neither let it be afraid."**

He also left us the Holy Spirit, who is our guide into all truth, and our comforter. Carmen also left us a powerful legacy in the earth to be a blessing to us all as well! She was a member of The Called and Ready Writers, and she authored two books; the first one was called, *How to Get your Groove Back*.

It is a book that was designed to be a practical guide to developing and maintaining an intimate fellowship with God.

The other book was entitled *Awaking Love*, which is the diary of a 45-year-old virgin, written in 2009. It is a must-read for those who have chosen to maintain their virginity until marriage by God's divine design. These two powerful, insightful, life-changing books have greatly blessed all who have had the privilege of reading them. She also collaborated with her sister Cynthia (who is a very anointed musician) to record a powerful healing CD of some of her favorite scriptures on healing. It was set to a beautiful background musical arrangement created by her sister.

I will never forget the day that she recorded this CD. She asked me to come over and support her with my presence and prayers while she created it. You would not believe the pain and suffering that I know she was experiencing, as she recorded it for the glory of God.

As I sat there watching and praying for her, you would have never known (while looking at her countenance) that she was in terrible pain. I know now that it could have been nothing but God's amazing grace upon her to fulfil His will. His strength was being made perfect in weakness, just as the scriptures have said (2 Corinthians 12:9).

Wow! What a blessing, privilege and an honour it was to be with her in the awesome presence of the Lord. Not to mention what it was like to see the power of the Holy Spirit moving her along, as He unfolded through her voice the revelation of His Word for those yet to hear. It was a moment in time that still impacts my life, even unto this very day. To be a witness to the power and supernatural strength of His grace, working in and through her, was something to behold!

What else can I say, but that it was absolutely

121

amazing!

Carmen's Personal Testimony

I thought you might enjoy reading a short excerpt of Carmen's testimony and legacy about why she wrote the book, *How to Get Your Groove Back*, especially because she was so passionate about prayer and helping people to understand its importance. Here is what she said:

"When I became a Christian, I heard people talking about praying and the importance of spending time with God. It made sense to me but I did not have a clue about how to begin that type of relationship. I read the salvation scripture, and knew I had a relationship with God through Christ but did not know how to fellowship with Him. I liken this to my childhood friend whom I called my boyfriend, but we never spent any time together. It also reminds me of the biblical story of the Prodigal Son in St. Luke 15th chapter, who had a relationship with his father, but did not seem to have fellowship with him.

When I began my journey with the Lord, trying to get to know Him was kind of awkward and intimidating for me. I thought, "Where do I begin? God is too big. He is too holy! Me? No way can I be cool with God." I thought only special people, like the pastor or priest, had access to God on a daily basis.

However, the scriptures boldly declare that we have access to God by faith through our Lord and Savior, Jesus Christ!

God desires fellowship and spending time with us beyond our wildest dreams. God is not desperate but, by His design, He wants to spend time with us. That's the groovy part!

My life has been transformed by God as I passionately spend time with Him on a daily basis. This simple yet powerful key has impacted my life and the lives of so many others. There is a saying that you are who you hang around. I believe as we study God's Word, spend time in prayer, and worship the Lord (daily) we are conformed to His image and walk out His original plan for our life. It is my prayer that as you read this book, you will get a revelation of God's love for you and His desire to manifest himself to you daily. Besides, He longs to be with you. Quiet as it is kept, you long to be with Him as well.

Many thought this book was about someone having a juicy relationship with a significant other. Well, it is. However, this groove is much deeper, more satisfying and long-lasting. This groove is with the Bishop of your soul, the one and only King of kings, Lord of lords, and so much more." 13

Having said all of this concerning Carmen's legacy, this was not all she left behind. To be so young, she was the wisest person I have ever known.

What I loved about the way she handled the revelation of scripture, was her dynamic ability to make it—practical. Perhaps I will just call it what she use to call it. She would say, "*We need to make it doable.*" I use to laugh with her as we discussed if that word could be found in the dictionary.

What she meant when she would use that word was, that we needed to learn to make the scriptures something we could *live out* by faith on an everyday basis, rather than something that just remained on the pages of scripture; with no practical application.

She knew how to make the scriptures so down to earth. I think it was an amazing gift being the teacher that she was in the body of Christ. She wanted people to be able to walk away (after having heard the revelation of scripture) with an action plan. How are we going to respond by the grace of God now that we have heard this lesson? This was the point she was seeking to make, because she was *committed* to being a doer of the Word and not a hearer only (James 1:22).

She could give such wise advice about how to live everyday life. She also wasn't afraid to tell you if she thought you needed to repent of something you had said or done. I can remember so many times on the phone with her, when we would be praying, that she would repent (on behalf of both of us) just in case we had said or done anything that might hinder our prayers in any way. Then I would agree with her. She always quoted this scripture to me saying, "*Ron, 'the goodness of God leads us to repentance' (Rom.2:4).*"

She didn't want anything standing between her fellowship and communion with the Father. She understood that God is holy and did not want to do anything to offend His holiness. She had a very sacred relationship and intimacy with Him and she knew it.

She did not want to take the covenant she had

with him for granted. This was another one of the many things I just loved about her.

Though space would not permit me to tell you all of the areas of legacy Carmen left us in the earth, I did feel the need to share a few of them.

After she passed I really began to think more seriously about leaving another legacy in the earth, and this new book is another part of mine. I feel passionate about this book and the opportunity to help others through the grieving process, just like God helped me. I can't say enough about how He continues to give me His grace day by day as I seek to finish my course with joy in this life, just as she finished hers.

Throughout our Christian journey here on earth, we certainly have gained some wisdom that I am sure can be passed down in many different forms by using our God-given creativity. Things like books, journals of your thoughts and prayer time spent with God, artwork, music, pictures, DVDs, or YouTube videos. How about some of your secret recipes of that delicious cooking you have done over the years! Does it still have to remain a "secret" recipe after you are gone? Someone is just waiting to get in on those secret recipes you made.

It may also be poetry you wrote that needs to be put into book form. What about a business the Lord blessed you with, as well? We can also impart the beliefs and values that we have held so dear of how we first accepted Christ as our Lord and Savior, or how we received a miraculous healing of a disease.

That's called your testimony, and we all have one for sure. That's how we overcome, by the blood of the Lamb and the word of our testimony (Rev. 12:11). All of these things together will serve like a roadmap does—to help show the coming generations the way.

The thing I love about legacy, perhaps the most, is that what we leave behind can help to "stabilize" the next generation who are going to have to live their lives in the midst of an "unstable" fallen world. We are living in the last days according to the scriptures and things are getting worse and worse, as the scriptures already said they would, before Jesus returns.

The generations to come will need faith, courage, and much confidence in God to make it in the days ahead, and to represent the Lord well in the earth by living a life that pleases God. This is our "opportunity" to help them do just that, so don't procrastinate! Don't keep putting it off until "tomorrow." You know how we tend to make excuses by "deferring" and "delaying" what God has been prompting us to do by His Spirit, don't you? We have done this for far too long! Let's not do this anymore as believers; let's be determined to finish strong! Do something for the glory of God! Leave a—legacy!

A Legacy of Faith

There is one more important legacy that I did not mention yet in detail. My pastor was preaching on New Year's Day, as we entered the year 2017. He mentioned "A Legacy of Faith" in his sermon. The text my pastor, Bishop Middleton, came from was 2 Timothy 1:5-12. I became so excited as he began to expound upon this message, as I realized that this would be something wonderful to add to this chapter of my book. Here are some of the thoughts I got out of what he said. It caused me to reflect back on how I grew up in the Roberson household.

A legacy of faith is about what we have received from the life of faith that others have lived before us, like the life of faith that my parents lived before me. When I was growing up we had "family devotions" around the dining room table. My father and mother would get their bibles, and my daughter and I would join them at the table.

We would sing old songs that my father had learned back in Augusta, Georgia, where he once lived. We would also pray, and read the scriptures on a regular basis. I had no idea at the time that they were leaving us a legacy of their faith and trust in God. They were imparting their love for God, a love for the scriptures and songs that spoke of His power and love —into our lives. It was a mighty impartation indeed!

Not only that, but they took us to church. They did not just send us, rather they became the *model* of the importance of not forsaking the assembly of the saints (Heb. 10:25). They were taking us to the church, which was "a community of faith" that was shaping our lives, and we didn't even know it at the time. They would testify in church to the goodness of the Lord before the congregation of the saints. They would praise God, clap their hands and pat their feet to the music.

All of this was their legacy of faith, being left to their loved ones. They wanted us to know God and to believe in Him with all our hearts, just like they did. They were trusting God to make Himself real in our lives, by planting the "initial seeds" needed to jumpstart our journey to knowing the one true and living God.

I cannot tell you how this legacy of faith has impacted my life, even until this very day. Not only my life but my daughter's life and my grandson's too.

My daughter loves the Lord and is a true worshipper. She also ministers on the praise team at our local church. My grandson is a minister of the gospel of Jesus Christ and loves God with his whole heart—and it all stemmed from the impact that my parents' *legacy of faith* has had on all of our lives. So, even though you may not be a book writer, a song writer, a singer or any of those type of things, you can always leave a legacy of "faith" for the generations to come. What will be your legacy?

Leaving Your Legacy?

I want to leave a few lines now, to give you space to record your legacy that you will leave in the earth, when you leave this expression of life. We will all leave sooner or later to be with our Lord and Savior, Jesus Christ, which is not something to "dread" but something to look forward to, ultimately. I am sure that I am not original when I say this, but I think we need to learn to see death more as a transitional moment, rather than some terrible dreaded end that we spend our whole lives fearing. We need to think of death more like going to "sleep" in Jesus.

That said, I don't want any of us to be too hasty (at the same time) about wanting to get up out of here, as we see everything being shaken in this world; that can be shaken. Just because it's "shaking" does not mean it is our time to depart. Some of us already have our bags packed and have been standing at the bus station of life (like my pastor would sometimes say), just waiting to get out of this troubled world in order to escape the shaking. Regarding the fear of death, this is what the bible says in Hebrew 2:14, 15:

> **"Forasmuch then as the children are partakers of flesh and blood, he also himself likewise took part of the same; that through death he might destroy him who had the power of death, that is the devil; and deliver them who through fear of death were all their lifetime subject to bondage."**

I want to encourage you to unpack those bags and calm down. We have so much work yet to do, so much legacy to release, so many souls yet to be saved, so please don't lose your focus!

The bible tells us it is shaking, so that what cannot be shaken shall remain (Heb. 12:27). We must survive the shaking until we have completed our assignment in the earth. So, since we have been allotted this time by God, then it's a good time to think about what blessing we will leave in the earth.

God had something in mind when He created you and, as my pastor says so well, *"we don't have a right to leave the planet without fulfilling it."* So, I want you to think seriously now about what God has done in your life. What do you have in you that can be left as a legacy for your family, and for others that you may leave behind. What will yours be? If you feel uncertain about this, just ask God. He invited us in the book of James to ask for wisdom if we lack it (James 1:5). He's just waiting for you to ask!

Your Legacy Notes: Write out your commitment to leave a legacy in the earth, right here!

_____

_____

_____

_____

_____

_____

_____

_____

_____

_____

_____

_____

_____

_____

_____

CHAPTER 16

THE BLOOD STILL WORKS!

"But when they came to Jesus and found that he was already dead, they did not break his legs. Instead, one of the soldiers pierced Jesus' side with a spear, bringing a sudden flow of blood and water."

John 19:33, 34 (NIV)

"Surely he hath borne our griefs, and carried our sorrows: yet we did esteem him stricken, smitten of God, and afflicted. But he was wounded for our transgressions, he was bruised for our iniquities: the chastisement of our peace was upon him; and with his stripes we are healed."

Isaiah 53:4-5

Now, let's move on to the subject of the powerful shed blood of our Lord and Saviour, Jesus Christ. I suspect that, for some people, there just may be a little elephant in the room when it comes to this issue of "divine healing." The elephant in the room that we all see, but may not be talking about, is concerning *the truth* about the blood of Jesus Christ.

It seems at times when someone leaves this expression of life, after we have declared and believed for their healing (like we did for Carmen), that some may find themselves questioning in their subconscious minds about whether the blood still works. We just can't seem to understand what could have possibly happened. It is such a mystery.

Why did our loved ones still die, even after we prayed, fasted, and believed God? Of course, we may never express all of these concerns to the Lord or even to others because we don't want to offend the holiness of our God, seeing He knows and hears all things. However, this nagging thought about the blood may still remain hidden somewhere in our minds—even if we choose to never verbalize it.

Of course, the devil is going to say it didn't work because the person died. He thinks that's proof that the blood didn't work. He is seeking to *deceive* us by putting this lie on display in our minds, to torment us like a nagging headache would do. Therefore, he thinks he has won that battle. After all, he will whisper in our ear, *"you pleaded the blood of Jesus in faith over that person and they still died, didn't they*? I hope you will not buy into this lie; after all John 8:44 does tell us that the devil is a liar and the truth is not in him. In fact, the bible says he is the father of lies—as in the "founding father" of lies—so how can we expect anything he says to be true?

Just think about this. How can the devil win a battle that has already been fought and won at the cross? Therefore, the only place he has left to try and win a battle is in our *minds*. That's why we have to "govern," i.e., protect how we think, and cast down imaginations that are contrary to the truth of scripture (2 Corinthians 10:4-5). Let's not spend all our time "listening" to those lies but rather be seekers of the truth that makes us free (John 8:32). Where can we find the truth? It's in the Word of God!

What is true is what the scriptures say (which must always be our focus) as believers—in Christ. The Bible is our standard for faith and practice in all things. Therefore, we must not exalt our personal experience over the revelation of scripture, no matter how we feel about the outcome.

It is always the believer's job to "believe," and to "declare" that belief out of our mouths according to our God-given authority in Christ! The outcome is always in the hands of the Sovereign Lord, who has the big picture of it all; and we ultimately must admit that we do not. We must accept the truth, that He is God and we are not.

The truth is also that we don't fully know the state that our loved ones may have been in at the point of death. There have been times when some believers have asked to go home or have chosen to go and be at home with the Lord, for reasons that may be unknown to us. They may be tired of fighting or being in pain, or it could be for any other number of reasons. They may have just decided that they are ready to meet the Lord, even though they may not choose to share that with us. They may be trying to just hang on in there, because we want them to. We just don't know! Our understanding has limitations on it.

These are the type of things that we may be totally unaware of at times, but God knows all things. In His wisdom, he may either *allow* or *choose* to bring them home, according to His *perfect* or *permissive* will. Only God knows the end from the beginning of a thing. Jesus said *"I am the Alpha and the Omega, the beginning and the ending"* (Revelations 1:8). Our knowledge of these things is sometimes limited. One thing is for sure, it is a serious test of our faith when God doesn't do what we hoped and prayed that He would do.

Sometimes God chooses to reveal the reasons to us, and sometimes He may not. We must learn to be okay with that because He is—God! What has been revealed unto us is that our healing was won for us at the cross. Therefore, by Jesus Christ and the stripes he bore on the cross (shedding his own blood), we are healed right now! Nothing can ever change that. Praise God! In 1 Peter 2:24, it says,

>"Who his own self bare our sins in his own
>body on the tree, that we, being dead to sins,
>should live unto righteousness: by whose
>stripes ye were healed."

(This is written in past tense).

Now, whether God chooses to *manifest* our healing in this life or the next is not in our hands. Either way, we are healed and made whole; that's the important thing to understand! In heaven, there is no sickness, no disease of any kind. So, when we get there, we will experience complete and total healing (wholeness), if it has not fully manifested in this life.

We also experience complete and total healing in this earthy life, as well. We see it all through the scriptures as Jesus went about healing and delivering those who were oppressed by the devil, as He journeyed through this expression of life (Acts 10:38; Matt. 4:23). There are millions of testimonies in our present day as well, of the miracles of healing and deliverance. There are far more healings in this life than can ever be counted. Some have even died and been brought back to life, and lived on for many years after that. The Bible says, "all things are possible" to them that believe (Matt. 19:26).

The issue of healing has already been settled for us, but when it will manifest is perhaps more of the issue we grapple with the most. Sometimes we get stuck between what my pastor calls, *"faith answering time and faith manifestation time."* That's when we must fight the good fight of faith until the end (I Tim. 6:12). It's when we are in the *middle* of it.

Faith answering time is *when* we pray. We believe we receive when we pray, but faith manifestation time isn't until our healing, or whatever we are standing in faith for, shows up.

In the meantime, we must hold fast to the confession of our faith without wavering, for He is faithful that promised (Heb. 10:23).

Here's the other important thing about addressing the elephant in the room. I know that not everyone believes in the devil or satan, as he is sometimes referred to in scripture. Although some may say they do not believe in his existence or in demons, if you believe that the bible is true; then you absolutely must believe that satan exists.

In the bible, there is a scripture where Jesus makes a direct reference to satan in His response to the leaders of His day. He had just healed a woman who had an infirmity for eighteen years, and the leaders wanted to argue with Him about why He healed her on the Sabbath day. This was a part of Jesus' response to them:

> **"And ought not this woman, being a daughter of Abraham, whom Satan hath bound, lo, these eighteen years, be loosed from this bond on the sabbath day."**
>
> **Luke 13:16**

Jesus clearly said in this text from the bible, *"whom Satan hath bound."* I needed to bring this up, because some people die from demonic attacks launched against them from our very real enemy—satan—which I will elaborate more on in the chapter called, "A Follower of Christ." We must be clear that sickness and disease does not come from God and, therefore, we must continue to offer "resistance" to these—demonic attacks!

The bible tells us to submit ourselves to God and resist the devil, and he must flee from us (James 4:7).

These points that I am making are all just to remind us that there are numerous reasons that cause people to leave this life early or even in some very terrible ways, but this still does not mean that the blood does not work. So, whether we receive our "manifestation" of healing in this life, or the next, we are still healed! Thank God!

As people of *faith*, our assignment is to continue to declare, decree, announce and proclaim our healing. We are also to declare healing for others who are experiencing sickness and disease in their bodies, and expect the manifestation to come forth. We must continue to lay hands on the sick and declare their recovery by faith (Mark 11:23-24). That's what the early church did, and many supernatural healings took place through the demonstration of their faith!

I remember one time when Bishop Middleton was preaching, he told us the story in the bible about Paul, who was stoned and dragged outside the city and left for dead. His persecutors thought he was dead because they had beaten him just that bad. Then, guess what the saints did? They surrounded Paul, the Lord raised him up, and he went right on fulfilling his assignment in the earth (Acts 14:19-22)! This is another must-read!

We, as believers in Jesus Christ, have that same "authority" and power as well. We need to "surround" our brothers and sisters in Christ like a shield, and back the devil up off of them—in Jesus name (John 14:13)! We serve the God of the "resurrection" and He is able to raise us up, for His glory in the earth! We have the power to call things that be not as though they were (Rom. 4:17).

We are also to use "wisdom" in how we govern our physical bodies as stewards, being trusted by God to exercise *discipline* and *balance*.

This means watching what we eat, getting proper exercise, and drinking enough water, as well, so we can live long, healthy lives and fulfil our dominion assignment in the earth (Gen. 1:26-28).

I believe we would see far more manifestations in this life if we learn to continue in his Word, which is proof that we are His disciples (John 8:31). The provision of healing at the cross must be appropriated (accessed) by faith. That's why we not only believe in the healing power of God in our hearts, but we also speak it forth out of our mouths with—boldness! We say by faith, *"by Jesus' stripes we are healed!"* We do this no matter how we feel because we are not looking at what is seen in the natural, but we are looking at unseen things in an unseen realm (2 Cor. 4:18).

What this means is that we see ourselves already healed (based on the revelation of scripture)—not by our earthly experience, or how we feel in our physical bodies. We see ourselves with nothing missing and nothing broken in this supernatural realm. We should see our loved ones that way too!

One of the scriptures I love so much, and seek to keep myself reminded of often (about life and death issues), is Romans 14:7-9, and this is what it says:

> **"For none of us liveth to himself and no man dieth to himself. For whether we live, we live unto the Lord; and whether we die, we die unto the Lord: whether we live therefore, or die, we are the Lord's.**
>
> **For to this end Christ both died, and rose, and revived, that he might be Lord both of the dead and living."**

In other words, we can't lose! Either way, we are the Lord's! That sounds like a win-win situation to me! We just cannot lose!

Wow! That's powerful, as Carmen use to say when she heard some awesome revelation of scripture. While I was writing this, and thinking about the power of the blood of Jesus, I suddenly remembered another scripture that the Lord gave to Carmen (when she almost died once before), and it is so powerful! She started hemorrhaging all of a sudden from an unknown source at the time, and she ended up in the emergency room. This is the verse the Lord gave her, as she went through that terrible time:

> **And when I passed by thee, and saw thee polluted in thine own blood, I said unto thee when thou wast in thy blood, Live; yea, I said unto thee when thou wast in thy blood, Live.**
>
> **Ezekiel 16:6**

Through this scripture, God said to her, I saw you when you were polluted in your own blood, and He said **live**. And guess what? She lived through that experience! It was nothing but the blood of Jesus!

Remember this: whether we live or die, as believers in Jesus Christ, we are the Lord's. This means that our life is in the hands of the Lord, *not* the hands of the devil. Yes! We already have the victory through our Lord, Jesus Christ! Rest assured that the blood still works!

Through the shed blood of Jesus, we that are believers:

- Have the forgiveness of all our sins (Heb. 9:22). Heb. 7:27, i.e., our sins have been remitted through the blood of Jesus. There is no more guilt and condemnation for those of us who are in Christ Jesus (Rom. 8:1). He died once and for all. Rev. 1:5 says that he loved us and washed us from our sins in His own blood.

140

- We receive a continual cleansing from sin (I John 1:9-7). Thank God for the cleansing from all unrighteousness!

- We have had our conscience purged from dead works to serve the living God (Heb. 9:13, 14). Now, we have the freedom to work because we *are* saved, rather than trying to work to *be* saved—which is impossible!

- We can draw near to God in faith because of the blood of Jesus (Heb. 10:19, 22). We now have an "open invitation" to approach a holy God, with freedom and confidence, because of the blood of Jesus!

- We overcome satan by the blood of the lamb and the word of our testimony (Rev. 12:11).

- We are sanctified through the shed blood of Jesus (Heb. 13:12).

- We have protection through the blood of Jesus. He is our **Passover lamb.** *"When I see the blood, I will pass over you"* (Exodus, chapter 12; 1 Cor. 5:7; John 1:29; 1 Pet. 1:19; Heb. 4:15; Mark 14:12; Heb. 12:24).

- We are healed through the blood of Jesus (Isaiah, chapter 53). He was wounded for our transgressions...and by His stripes we are healed!

Through the finished work of Jesus Christ on the cross, we have all of these benefits, and much more! We already have the victory over death, hell and the grave, through our Lord and Savior, Jesus Christ! It's already done!

In I Corinthians 15:52-58, it says concerning our victory in Christ over death:

"In a moment, in the twinkling of an eye, at the last trump: for the trumpet shall sound, and the dead shall be raised incorruptible, and we shall be changed. For this corruptible must put on incorruption and this mortal, must put on immortality. Then shall be brought to pass the saying that is written, Death is swallowed up in victory.

O death, where is thy sting? O grave, where is thy victory? The sting of death is sin; and the strength of sin is the law. But thanks be to God, which giveth us the victory through our Lord Jesus Christ. Therefore, my beloved brethren, be ye steadfast, unmovable, always abounding in the work of the Lord, forasmuch as you know that your labour is not in vain in the Lord."

It is my prayer, after you have now read this, that you will be more convinced than ever that—the blood still works! There is just no doubt about it! Thank God for the blood of Jesus, it will never lose its power!

CHAPTER 17

I'M A WINNER!

"Yea doubtless, and I count all things but loss for the excellency of the knowledge of Christ Jesus my Lord: for whom I have suffered the loss of all things, and do count them but dung, that I may win Christ."

Philippians 3:8

"That I may know him, and the power of his resurrection, and the fellowship of his sufferings, being made conformable to his death; If by any means I might attain unto the resurrection of the dead."

Philippians 3:10-11

One day I heard Carmen's mother say that shortly before she passed from this expression of life, she declared these words out loud: *"I'm a winner."* When she made this confession, she was very sick and her earthly life was rapidly coming to a close. I remember my heart just leaping for joy when I heard her mother say what Carmen boldly declared out of her mouth!

Wow! I was thinking to myself, what a powerful declaration of faith in God. Where does this kind of perspective come from in the midst of such adversity? In the midst of pain, trials and tribulation, she declared that she was a—winner!

This reminds me of a sermon my earthly father (Rev. Albert Roberson Sr.) preached before he left this expression of life.

He entitled his message, "We're on the Winning Side." It was the most powerful sermon I had ever heard him preach, but what did he mean by that? It was drawn like water from a well within him. It flowed out from the certainty that he knew deep down in his born-again spirit.

He knew that from the very day that he had received Jesus Christ as his personal Lord and Savior, that he had joined the winning side. He knew that Jesus was a winner. Therefore, if he joined himself to Jesus, then he would be on the winning side too! What made Jesus a winner?

Jesus had humbly submitted himself unto the will of the Father, and thereby had abolished death and brought immortality to light through the gospel (2 Timothy 1:10). This made it possible for us to receive eternal life. How can you lose when you have received the gift of eternal life? When you join yourself unto the Lord by receiving Him, you are one with Him now, and in the life to come. So this means that where He is you will be also one of these days. The bible says, "but he that is joined unto the Lord is one spirit" (I Corinthians 6:17).

You see, eternal life begins when you receive Christ as Lord! It is a gift that He gives you to live forever with Him. You can see this clearly in John 17:3, where Jesus said himself,

> **"And this is life eternal, that they might know thee the only true God, and Jesus Christ, whom thou hast sent."**

So, to know the Father and the Son is eternal life. We come to know the Father through Jesus Christ, because Jesus said *"no man comes to the Father, but by me"* (John 14:6).

Now, knowing this truth and being able to declare it in the face of the devil, who has come to intimidate you with the possibility of death, is a whole different thing altogether. It takes courage to make a bold declarative statement like that. Where do you get that kind of perspective of your life, and the grace to speak it with confidence, out loud?

An Eternal View

One time a precious woman of God that Carmen and I have known for years was asked to bring a word from the Lord at our monthly outreach meeting. She was a part of our mission fellowship at Mt. Zion, and her name is Sister Earlene McDonald. She is a very mature woman in the faith who had suffered some unspeakable things in her life, and yet she was always so positive and had a smile on her face whenever you saw her. Carmen and I always had so much respect for her, and the good fight of faith we always saw her living out before us as younger women in the faith.

When she got up to speak, she said her message was about having "An Eternal View." It was such a powerful expression of her faith, confidence and trust in God. Carmen and I sat there along with others from our team, just soaking in this "rhema" word of a higher perspective of life. It was a way of seeing life through the eyes of faith—not according to our natural eyesight, but from our born-again spirits.

It was born out of the "new birth" that Jesus spoke to Nicodemus about in John, chapter 3. It was based on being born from above, because of what Christ had done for us when He saved us. Our spirits had become "alive" unto God, and out of our spirits we could now see life from a higher and different point of view. It was from God's vantage point.

Though we already knew this on one level, the Lord used this woman of God to open this revelation up for us in a greater way. It was through her own personal experience of—knowing God intimately. It was learning to declare what you see from above, rather than what your experience dictates to you upon the earth. Carmen and I were just looking at each other and saying, *Wow!* as the truth was being released to us. We talked about it later on the phone and thanked God for that mighty impartation.

It is the kind of perspective that says things like *"to live is Christ, to die is to gain"* just like the apostle Paul said in Philippians 1:21. It is always in agreement with what the Word of God says, not how we feel. It comes out of knowing who you are in Christ! You must know clearly who you are in Christ to make these faith-filled affirmations. It is in Christ that we get our true identity. If you want to understand more clearly who you are in Christ, I highly recommend Neil T. Anderson's book, *Who I Am in Christ*. Carmen and I just loved this book. It is powerful!

Also, Carmen and I loved so much what Nelson Mandela said in his inauguration speech, as it relates to who we are and how we conduct ourselves in this life. That's why I felt compelled to put a part of his speech in **Appendix D** for you to read. You see, the devil cannot "define" us as believers in Jesus Christ by our circumstances or our physical condition, when we know who we are in Him!

Carmen knew who she was in Christ, and that's why she could say," *I'm a Winner."* She was speaking out of her *position* in Christ, not out of how it looked. The bible says in Ephesians 2:6, that we are *"seated together with Christ in heavenly places."* This is a reference to our position in Christ.

She was speaking "positional truth," not according to the doctor's diagnosis or what the devil had to say, but out of who she was in Christ!

No doubt, when she boldly uttered these words, the devil may have been whispering that she was a loser, because that is what liars do. It is all a part of the battlefield of the mind that we all experience. However, she knew the truth—that to be absent from the body was to be present with the Lord (2 Corinthians 5:8)! Now she is present and accounted for in heaven, as a true child of God! Yes! Carmen was and still is a—winner!

This revelation of who we are in Christ was so important to both Carmen and I. We had even talked about putting something together on CD on this topic of who we are, but we ran out of time. That's why I included a chart in this book in **Appendix C,** so you could *meditate* and *affirm* who you are in Christ from these powerful passages of scripture.

I know as you take the time to begin to affirm these truths in your own life, that you will gain so much assurance that when the devil comes to intimidate you, you will be able to declare who you are in Christ in the midst of it all. It's how you learn to live life above the sun rather than under the sun. A new day will dawn in your life, when you begin to release these truths into the atmosphere that surrounds you! It will be the beginning of a turning point, and a new day in your life for sure!

CHAPTER 18

THE LAST ENEMY

Then cometh the end, when he shall have delivered up the kingdom to God, even the Father; when he shall have put down all rule and all authority and power. For he must reign, till he hath put all enemies under his feet. The last enemy that shall be destroyed is death."

1 Corinthians 15:24-26

Death is swallowed up in victory. O death, where is thy sting? O grave, where is thy victory? The sting of death is sin; and the strength of sin is the law. But thanks be to God, which gives us the victory through our Lord Jesus Christ.

I Corinthians 15:54b-57

What is an enemy? According to *Vine's Expository Dictionary of Biblical Words*, an enemy denotes *hated or hateful. Hating, or hostile, adversary and is said of the Devil.*[14] Matt.13:39; Luke 10:19. The bible tells us that death is an enemy referred to as "the last enemy," and it tells us that a day is coming that death itself will be destroyed. Praise God!

I'm just saying this as a reminder that death is not a "friend" but an "enemy" to us, and one day we will be free from death and the very presence of evil. Can you imagine that? One day, there will be no more funerals to attend! No more crying over the loss of loved ones either. What a day of rejoicing that will be!

Fear of Death All Their Lifetime

There is a powerful scripture I think I mentioned to you before, in Hebrews 2:14-15, speaking of Jesus and it says:

> "Forasmuch then as the children are partakers of flesh and blood, he also himself likewise took part of the same; that through death he might destroy him that had the power of death, that is the devil; and delivered them who through fear of death were all their lifetime subject to bondage."

Wow! That's awesome! The devil *had* the power of death, and everyone was in bondage (all their lifetime) to the devil, and had fear of death until Jesus came and delivered us from the bondage of the fear of death. Now we no longer have to live our lives in fear of death! Hebrews 2:9 tells us that Jesus tasted death for every man. It says:

> "But we see Jesus, who was made a little lower than the angels, for the suffering of death, crowned with glory and honour; that he by the grace of God should taste death for every man."

When Jesus took on humanity (flesh and blood) to die for us, He gave all mankind the "opportunity" to receive the gift of eternal life with God. All of this was necessary because Romans 5:12 says,

> "Wherefore, as by one man sin entered into the world, and death by sin: and so death passed upon all men, for that all have sinned."

While all of us are so heartbroken when our loved ones pass on, we must remind ourselves that this enemy (called death) is under Jesus' feet according to the scriptures, and therefore under ours too! It won't always be this way. We need not fear death, because Jesus has already taken care of that for us. We need to focus rather on life!

We must live our lives to the fullest while we are still here. We must enjoy our lives even in the absence of our loved ones. We must not fret and grieve forever. God did not intend for us to live our lives like that. He said, "I came that you might have life and that more abundantly" (John 10:10). We cannot change what has already happened, and our being sad and depressed won't change anything.

Let's take a moment to see if we can glean some insights from how Joshua handled the death of Moses, Israel's spiritual leader in the wilderness. I can only imagine the bond between Moses and Joshua as leaders of the tribe of Israel. In the bible, when Moses died Joshua had to "adjust" to going on without him.

This must have been such a sad time for Joshua, especially since Moses was his leader, traveling companion and beloved friend. Joshua was loyal to him, worked closely with him, and ministered unto him faithfully from his youth (Num. 11:28). Listen to what God told Joshua after Moses had died and he had been chosen by God to be the next leader of the children of Israel:

In Joshua 1:1-3 it says,

"Now after the death of Moses the servant of the LORD it came to pass, that the LORD spake unto Joshua the son of Nun, Moses' minister, saying, Moses my servant is dead;

> now therefore arise, go over this Jordan,
> thou, and all this people, unto the land which
> I do give to them, even to the children of
> Israel. Every place that the sole of your foot
> shall tread upon, that have I given unto you,
> as I said unto Moses."

Then over in verse 5 of the same chapter, God says to Joshua:

> As I was with Moses, so I will be with thee: I
> will not fail thee, nor forsake thee. Be strong
> and of good courage...".

Therefore, I say the same thing to you now. Be strong and of good courage, as God was with your loved one, so he will be with you. God is faithful and He promised! I close this chapter with one of my many favorite scriptures, found in Isaiah 41:10 (AMP):

> "Fear not [there is nothing to fear], for I am
> with you; do not look around in terror and be
> dismayed, for I am your God. I will
> strengthen and harden you to difficulties,
> yes, I will help you; yes, I will hold you up
> and retain you with My [victorious] right
> hand of rightness and justice."

CHAPTER 19

A FOLLOWER OF CHRIST

"For even hereunto were ye called: because Christ also suffered for us, leaving us an example, that ye should follow his steps: who did no sin neither was guild found in his mouth…"

I Peter 2:21

Then Jesus told His disciples, "if anyone would come after me, let him deny himself and follow me."

Matthew 16:24 (ESV)

That I may know him and the power of his resurrection and may share his sufferings, becoming like him in his death.

Phil. 3:10 (ESV)

There was an old song we use to sing in church, and the words went something like this: *"I want to be a follower of Christ. I want to be one of his disciples. I want to walk in the newness of life, so let me be a follower of Christ."* As the song went on, it came to a part that said, *"What does it cost to carry the cross?"* These words still ring out in my heart as I reflect on my precious friend Carmen, who suffered so much.

As I was coming to the close of this book, I was checking with God to make sure I had covered the areas that were on His heart.

I knew I couldn't cover it all, but I just wanted to be sure that I had tapped into His heart on this subject—to the extent that He wanted me to. That's when He dropped this chapter on me as He spoke with me about being a follower of Christ.

As I began to reflect back on this song I just spoke of, I began to think of the cost to carry the cross. I reflected upon Jesus' followers in the scripture and how most of them were killed for following Him. When Jesus first began to call His disciples, He would say to them *"follow me."* In some cases, some of the disciples He called were fishermen, and so Jesus would say to them "follow me, and I will make you fishers of men." However, first they had to be willing to follow, and that was not going to be without a price!

They were being called to be His witnesses "in the earth." One of the meanings of the word "witness" is "martyr." It describes someone who suffers persecution and death for following Christ. These are saints that died for being committed and faithful to the Lord. They were chosen channels to carry the message of the good news of the gospel of Jesus Christ, at home and abroad no matter the cost! They were to be loyal to their master even unto the point of death, if necessary.

There were also others outside of the original disciples—like Stephen—who were martyred for the faith once delivered to the saints. He was a true follower of Christ, who served as a deacon in the early church. Stephen was martyred for the faith by being stoned to death, for preaching the good news of the gospel of Jesus Christ. This is one of the most powerful scenes of someone in biblical times, being martyred for their belief and bold proclamations. I want to give you a portion of this text hoping you will read it in its entirety. Speaking of Stephen, the bible says in Acts 7:55-58:

> "But he, being full of the Holy Ghost, looked up steadfastly into heaven, and saw the glory of God, and Jesus standing on the right hand of God, and said, Behold, I see the heavens opened, and the Son of man standing on the right hand of God."

Did you hear that? It says Stephen saw Jesus standing on the right hand of God. That's awesome because in many other places in scripture it says Jesus is seated at the right hand of the Father (Hebrews 1:3; Colossian 3:1). But, wow, when He saw His servant being martyred for his commitment to Him—He stood up from His position of honor in the heavenlies! That's more awesome than I could ever elaborate on in a million years!

After Stephen said that, the text goes on to say, regarding the response of the people to Stephen's hard hitting message:

> "Then they cried out with a loud voice, and stopped their ears, and ran upon him with one accord, and cast him out of the city, and stoned him: and the witnesses laid down their clothes at a young man's feet, whose name was Saul."

After reminding myself of this powerful text, something else immediately came up in my mind. I was thinking, can we really be followers of Christ without carrying the cross? Actually, Jesus said, *"if any man will come after me let him deny himself, take up his cross, and follow me"* (Matt. 16:24). When you search back through the history of the disciples of Jesus Christ, you will find out that they were mostly martyred for the faith in some very cruel ways, indeed.

155

When we think of the "cross," we can hardly help but think of pain, suffering, and death, which nobody likes to think about these days—more or less becoming a martyr. I don't really think anybody is rushing to be the first to line up for this type of persecution for the faith!

Modern Day Martyrs

These martyrs I have been speaking of were from a very long time ago, back in biblical days. This brings up the subject of modern-day martyrs. Are there still saints today that are being martyred? The answer to the question, which I already know you didn't want to ask, is absolutely yes! I think most of us would feel relieved to think that believers were only martyred way back then, because I'm sure nobody wants to be a martyr. Though it would make us feel better not to think this is happening now, it is truly not the case.

There are missionaries and evangelists right now on the mission fields who are being martyred right up to this very present day. It is so bad that there is even an organization that is called "The Voice of the Martyrs." It is an organization that is seeking to bring more attention to these suffering saints, as well as to support them in whatever way they can. They share in great detail some of the sufferings of the persecuted church, of which we are all members, since we are the body of Christ.

These saints are His "witnesses" who are sold out, and willing to do whatever it takes to preach the gospel to the lost. Some of them are even in prison right now due to "false accusations" made against them, and are now separated from their families for an indefinite period of time!

Some will even die in these prisons, be beheaded, or never get released.

I have had the pleasure of meeting one of them through this organization, who was *almost* martyred in China. What torture she experienced. Her testimony is incredible of the beatings and cruel treatment she received for sharing the gospel of Jesus Christ. I will not use her name, just in case, to protect her identity. She is an amazing saint of God who suffered persecution and imprisonment for the cause of Christ.

She has written several books about her experiences, which are so powerful to read! Thank God, through it all, she is still in the land of the living and sharing her testimony, wherever the Lord sends her, as a true follower of Jesus Christ! I feel so honoured to have met her personally!

This is also the kind of life that Carmen was committed to living. Among so many other things that Carmen was (as a child of God), she was truly a missionary-minded saint. She always sought to spread the good news wherever she went. She was passionate about being a soul winner for Christ! She ministered to children (whom she loved so very much) seeking to get them saved at an early age. She also worked with our Vacation Bible School in the past, doing fun things like being a clown and face painting, while witnessing to the little children.

She was on our evangelistic street team at Mt. Zion, walking the streets of our community, seeking to win lost souls to Christ through all four seasons of life. Carmen and I also had the opportunity to travel together to South Africa in August 2003, to share the good news of Jesus Christ. It also gave us a chance to enhance our awareness of people who have never heard the good news of the gospel. It was both a challenging and life-changing experience, indeed.

Once she realized the depth of the price that Jesus had paid for her life (because of his great love),

157

she wanted to share that love with everyone she met. She was what you call—sold out. From my perspective, she was a modern-day martyr, who paid the price to do her part to fulfil the great commission in Matthew 28:18-20, where Jesus says:

> **"All power is given unto me in heaven and in earth. Go ye therefore, and teach all nations, baptizing them in the name of the Father, and of the Son, and of the Holy Ghost: Teaching them to observe all things whatsoever I have commanded you: and lo, I am with you always, even unto the end of the world. Amen."**

She had "caught" the heart of the Father for *"every nation, tribe, people and language,"* to be saved through the gospel! As my pastor sometimes says, *"some things are better caught than taught."* It is clear that she loved not her life unto the death (Rev. 12:11). How amazing is that?

One thing is for sure, when you are serving the Lord you will be hated of all men. Jesus said that himself in Matthew 10:22. *"And ye shall be hated of all men for my name's sake; but he that endureth to the end shall be saved"* In I John 3:13 it says, *"marvel not, my brethren if the world hate you"*. This is to be expected, since they hated Jesus too. There are demon spirits assigned to destroy our lives, when they see the "nature" of Christ manifesting itself through us, as we impact the world for Jesus Christ—especially when our words are in alinement with our lifestyle. That's a winning combination!

The truth is, as we move more and more toward Christlikeness, we become more and more of a threat and a *target* for satan to aim his fiery darts at. We must lift up our shield of faith to quench those fiery darts, according to the scriptures.

That's why we are instructed to put on the whole armour of God, so we can stand against the wiles of the devil (Ephesians 6). Why would we need to do that, unless we are in a war? We must face the truth that we are in a WAR, or we wouldn't need all of the spiritual weapons that the bible speaks about.

The truth is, that we are soldiers in the army of the Lord (2 Tim. 2:3-5). Some of us are on the front line as "front line warriors" in the battle. Most of the time, when there is a battle there are "casualties." We can see that even from the natural wars that we have been in with others, as the United States of America. Many soldiers have lost their lives in war. We call them "fallen soldiers," and we also call them heroes for their amazing sacrifice.

Sometimes some of the saints get hit during spiritual battles, since this is the nature of war. Though satan is a "formidable" foe, we must keep ourselves reminded that he is already a "defeated" foe, as well (Colossians 2:15). We need not fear him since Jesus already defeated him at the cross. We must also *not retreat* from our assignment to *enforce* his defeat, because we got hit as the body of Christ! After all, as I once heard a wise man say, *"for us as believers it means sudden death, sudden glory!"*

Remember, we can't lose a battle that has already been fought and won! As in any war, it is so painful to lose a member of the redeemed community (from this expression of life) in the midst of the battle. However, we still must be determined to go forward together, and fulfil our corporate assignment in the earth.

We rest in the biblical revelation that we will see our brothers and sisters again—not as a fallen soldier, but in a far more "exalted state" when we get to heaven. Praise God! Until then, I encourage you to stay the course and finish strong!

CHAPTER 20

HAPPILY EVER AFTER

"Surely I come quickly. Amen. Even so, come, Lord Jesus."

Revelation 22:20

For no man can lay a foundation other than the one which is laid, which is Jesus Christ.

1 Corinthians 3:11 (NASB)

...having been built on the foundation of the apostles and prophets, Christ Jesus Himself being the corner stone.

Ephesians 2:20 (NASB)

When I was growing up, I wasn't that much of a reader, but I did end up with a few great children's books that held my interest! Most of them started off with "Once upon a time...," then it would go into the storyline, and finally on to my favorite part—the line that said *"and they lived happily ever after."* I just loved that part. When I opened the book, it had a big "O" on the page, and then the rest of the word (nce) added to it. Together, the sentence read—"Once upon a time." I could hardly wait to see what it was all about, from a child's perspective. My childhood love for mysteries, had begun!

The beginning of the book started so well, but as the storyline began to unfold, it would usually get pretty ugly in the middle—like the one about the three little pigs.

They were just three little pigs setting out on a new adventure to make a decent life for themselves. Unfortunately, two of them failed to take their mother's sound advice she had given them before they left home. She told them, *"Whatever you do, do the best that you can because that is the way to get along in the world."*[15] So, they went out to find some materials to build their house with. The first one built his house out of straw, the second one built his house out of sticks, and the third one built his house out of bricks.

That third pig was the wise one who remembered his mother's wise advice about doing the best you can. So, one night the big bad wolf (who loved to eat up little piggies) showed up and threatened to blow their house down one by one, so he could eat them up.

He started with the first little pig and he said to him, *"Let me in, let me in, little pig or I'll huff and puff and I'll blow your house in."*[16] This little pig made a bold affirmation in response to this threat saying, *"Not by the hair of my chinny chin chin."*[17] But because his house was made of straw, the wolf was able to blow it down, and the same thing with the second little pig because his house was made of sticks. Wow! At his point, it seemed to me that the big bad wolf was winning, which is creating major anxiety in my little young mind.

Right about now, I could feel myself starting to get uptight when I would get to this dramatic part of the story. With all this bad stuff happening I began to feel afraid, seeing I was only a child. I would get fearful and feel I just couldn't take the stress of it all. I would get so nervous wondering if the wolf would end up killing all those little pigs, or what! I just needed to be sure that things would turn out alright in the end.

That's why I would skip over some of the bad parts and read the end of the story. At the end of the book it said these words, which sounded like music to my ears: *"and they lived happily ever after."*[16] Then I would smile and start laughing, knowing all was going to be well in the end! I would take a deep breath (to release my childhood tension), and then I would begin to feel so much better. Then, I would go back and read the bad part and be okay with it, because I knew in the end that at least one of those three little pigs would win! Even though the other two did not make it, I was comforted that at least one of them did.

Once I became a young adult and began reading the bible with a greater understanding, I began to realize that this three-little-pig story seemed to have some slight similarities to a biblical story. In the bible, after the creation of the heaven and the earth (and many more details), it went on to tell the story of the first man and woman, named Adam and Eve.

Everything seemed to be going so well with them in their relationship with God. They also had a beautiful home environment in the garden of Eden, designed by God. But, then, things took a mighty bad turn. They disobeyed God and chose to listen to the voice of satan, disguised as the serpent. Things seemed to be going downhill really fast after that, for all of mankind. Then, at the appointed time, God sent His promised one and only Son, Jesus, to save us from our sins (Matt. 1:21; Eph. 2:1-7).

Although the enemy still keeps trying to blow our house down (so to speak) with sickness, disease, tragedy and the death of loved ones, and on and on, he will never be successful, since we have now accepted Christ as our personal Lord and Savior. We are now—in Christ, and He is our hiding place!

He is the rock of our salvation, therefore we (like the third little pig who built his house out of brick) are as solid as a rock! The house of our life is built—in Him. We are joined to the Lord and we are one in spirit with him (1 Corinthians 6:17). Our real life is now *"hidden with Christ in God"* (Colossians 2:15).

Is Your House Built Right?

Storms of life will come and winds will blow, but if our house is built right, it will still be standing on the other side of the storm. Every house that is built right has a solid foundation. It takes "time" to build a solid foundation to stand on to make it through the storms of life. If we rush though life without taking the time to lay the "foundation" properly, then when the rain and storms come we will not be able to stand, just like the house built on sand in the bible (Matt. 7:24-27). When the time of testing showed up for both houses, one passed the test and one did not, because it was not built right. It could not stand the pressure of hard times. How do you lay a proper foundation for your life, someone may be thinking?

I think I can best help you see what I mean by telling you the short version of how these foundation stones must be laid in every Christians life, in order to stand the storms of life. My former pastor had passed away and my new pastor was Bishop Charles Middleton. After he met us all and things had settled down some, he was now going to start us all on a new series of studies from some material he had written called "Foundations Stones." The class was titled, "The New Foundations Study Course." Those of us who were presently sitting under him had come from a ministry where we were mostly teachers, who had been studying the scriptures for many years.

Some of us were dreading to take this course, because the feeling was that we had learned all of this foundational stuff a long time ago. We thought we were a little too "mature" in the scriptures to go back to foundational truths, for sure. I am sure you can hear the "pride" in all of this, since the bible does say "knowledge puffeth up," right? (1 Cor. 8:1b).

Not only that, but our pastor went on to blow our natural minds when he said that the course was broken down into four sections, and that it was going to take us at least one to two years to complete it, in its entirety. That was a downer for sure from our perspective! So, anyway, we submitted ourselves to what he wanted us to do, with a lot of apprehension and a bit of dread too.

Then, when he passed the material out to us, and we began to study it from week to week, we began to think that this material was the "deepest" material we had ever seen, in all our years of study. Most of us were seriously struggling to pass each course. We were just hoping to make a good "C" at this point!

The lessons consisted of Repentance from Dead Works, Faith Toward God, and The Doctrines of Baptisms (Baptism into the Body of Christ, Baptism into Water, and Baptism into the Holy Spirit), The Laying on of Hands, The Resurrection of the Dead, and—last but not least—Eternal Judgment. This last lesson was a study from the book of Revelation, which most of us perceived to be the "deepest" book in the whole bible.

These were the foundation stones that he was seeking to lay in our lives. I just can't imagine what it was that made Bishop think that we had not already laid these foundation stones—properly.

Perhaps he sighted some level of "immaturity" in our "puffed up" reaction to this challenge. You think?

I soon got the message that these teachings were considered "foundational teachings" for the Christian life. It was then that I started laughing in a hilarious way, as I said to myself "You have got to be kidding? You mean these are "foundational teachings" as in "elementary school" teachings? These teachings are just the ABCs of the Christian faith? The reason I was laughing so hard was because I thought I had laid these a long time ago! I am sure that the rest of our class was thinking the same thing too! It was too funny!

Then he gave us the scripture that these foundation stones were taken from, and it was Hebrews 6:1-3, and here is what it says:

> **"Therefore, leaving the principles of the doctrine of Christ, let us go on unto perfection; not laying again the foundation of repentance from dead works, and of faith towards God, of the doctrines of baptisms, and of laying on of hands, and of resurrection of the dead, and of eternal judgment."**

It goes on to say:

> **"...And this we will do if God permit."**

Then, Bishop went on to inform us that God may not permit us to go on, if these stones were not properly laid. Why? This will take us right back to the story in the bible about the house built on a rock, and the house built on sand (Matt. 7:24-27). If our house is not built right, then the foundation of our lives will not be able to withstand the coming storms.

Therefore, we must learn these biblical truths, no matter how much time it takes, and put them into practice; in order to be able to stand against the wiles of the devil. I hope you got the message!

Many things, like the passing of loved ones, will come, and because satan is an opportunist, he will use these tough times to take advantage of our *vulnerabilities* and bring in a spirit of discouragement; making us feel a sense of defeat. Our adversary is like that big bad wolf trying to blow down the houses of the three little pigs. He is constantly threatening to bring our house down.

We will still have times in this life when we get discouraged, like during times of grief, and we may even feel like giving up from all the hardships and the contrary winds of life. However, we can still depend on Jesus as our solid rock. In times like these we can also go to the end of the book, and in essence it says at the end...and they lived happily ever after! We can start rejoicing about that right now! Our happily ever after, at the back of the book, reads like this from the New Living Translation (NLT) in Revelation 22:20:

> **"He who is the faithful witness to all these things says, Yes, I am coming soon! Amen! Even so come Lord Jesus! May the grace of the Lord Jesus be with God's holy people."**

Yes, the good news is that the bible ends with the promise of Jesus' return one day, to take us to our eternal home. If something happens to our earthly house down here, and this house of flesh is no longer able to sustain us, don't worry; we will not be "evicted" and end up "homeless." Why?

It's because we have another building to go to, that was not built with human hands, according to the scriptures (2 Cor. 5:1). Thank God!

It is a prepared place for a prepared people, and it is eternal in the heavens. This is our joyful hope and our constant expectation: that one of these days we will be with the one who saved us from our sins, whether we are still alive at the time, or have died in the Lord. We will be with Him! It sounds like happily ever after to me! I wanted to share this with you as a word of comfort, in thinking about seeing our loved ones again who have passed on at—the appointed time.

I just wanted to remind you that if you have a personal relationship with Jesus Christ, and your loved one(s) were saved, then you can be sure that there will be a wonderful reunion in heaven one of these old days. That's really going to be something to look forward to in God's perfect timing! In the meantime, enjoy these encouraging words from the book of Psalms. They give you encouragement to keep on thanking and praising God, for the rest of your journey.

The Book of Psalms

Whenever I read the book of Psalms, I can still hear Carmen saying to me, *"Wow Ron, the Psalms are really powerful."* It seemed kind of strange to me at the time that she would say this, since I happen to know that she had been reading the Psalms for years, but now I think I understand what she meant. She was in the hospital with a very bad diagnosis when she said these words to me. Therefore, she was now seeing these power scriptures with *fresh eyes.* It's like she had never read them before. You get fresh revelation of the scriptures when you approach them this way.

What I mean is that, when you go through different seasons of your journey (and you read the scriptures during one of those times), it seems like you are reading them for the first time in your life. That's just how relevant the scriptures really are in our everyday lives. She was reading the Psalms from a *transitional perspective*, as she was leaving one expression of life, to go to the next.

This kind of situation brings on a totally different perspective of the scriptures, I am sure. Thank God that the Word never grows old, and it always speaks a word in season to us just when we need it the most. We will always need to see these "sacred" writings with fresh eyes, in order to make it through the various seasons of our lives. This is my prayer in fact for you right now, that you will behold the Psalms with—fresh eyes.

Note: I would like to encourage you to read these scriptures from your bible, so you can get the full effect of each of these powerful verses. They are only listed here in part.

ENCOURAGING WORDS FROM THE BOOK OF PSALMS

"...but David encouraged himself in the Lord"
I Samuel 30:6

Psalm 5:3 – My voice shalt thou hear in the morning, O LORD...
Psalm 9:1-2 – I will praise thee, O LORD, with my whole heart...
Psalm 18:6-9 – In my distress I called upon the LORD and cried...
Psalm 18:17-18 – He delivered me from my strong enemy and...

Psalm 18:28-37 – For thou wilt light my candle; the LORD my God...

Psalm 19:14 – Let the words of my mouth, and the meditation of my...

Psalm 20:7 – Some trust in chariots, and some in horses: but we will...

Psalm 23 – The Lord is my shepherd I shall not want. He maketh me...

Psalm 24:7 – Lift up your heads, O ye gates; and be ye lifted up...

Psalm 27 – The Lord is my light and my salvation; whom shall I fear..

Psalm 29:11 – The Lord will give strength unto his people; the LORD

Psalm 30: 5, 11-12 – Weeping may endure for a night, but joy cometh...

Psalm 31:2-3 – Bow down thine ear to me; deliver me speedily; be...

Psalm 34:1, 8 – I will bless the LORD at all times: his praise shall...

Psalm 38:9 – Lord, all my desire is before thee; and my groaning is...

Psalm 40:1-3 – I waited patiently for the LORD; and he inclined...

Psalm 42:8 – Yet the LORD will command his lovingkindness in ...

Psalm 46:1, 10 – God is our refuge and strength, a very present help...

Psalm 46:10 – Be still and know that I am God: I will be exalted...

Psalm 48:14 – For this God is our God for ever and ever; he will be...

Psalm 55:16-18, 22 – As for me, I will call upon God; and the LORD

Psalm 56:3-4, 9-11 – What time I am afraid, I will trust in thee...

Psalm 61:1-3 – When my heart is overwhelmed; lead me to the rock...

Psalm 62:1-2, 5-8 – My soul, wait...for my expectation is from him...

Psalm 63:1-7 – thy loving kindness is better than life: my lips shall...

Psalm 64:1-2 – preserve my life from fear of the enemy. Hide me...

Psalm 69:16-17 – Hear me, O LORD; for thy lovingkindness is good

Psalm 71:1-3, 14 – O LORD, ... let me never be put to confusion

Psalm 73:24-26, 28 – Thou shall guide me with thy counsel, and ...

Psalm 77:1-14 – In the day of my trouble I sought the Lord: my ...

Psalm 90:12 – So teach us to number our days, that we may apply...

Psalm 91:1-16 – He that dwelleth in the secret place of the most High

Psalm 92:1-2 – It is a good thing to give thanks unto the LORD, ...

Psalm 100:1-5 – Make a joyful noise unto the LORD all ye lands...

Psalm 102:24 – I said, O my God, take me not away in the midst of...

Psalm 103:1-22 – Bless the LORD, O my soul; and all that is within...

Psalm 112:7-8 – He shall not be afraid of evil tidings: his heart is...

Psalm 113:3 – From the rising of the sun unto the going down of ...

Psalm 116:17 – I will offer to thee the sacrifice of thanksgiving, ...

Psalm 118:8, 17, 24 – It is better to trust in the LORD than to put...

Psalm 119:28 – My soul melts away for sorrow, strengthen me...

Psalm 119: 89, 105, 114 – For ever, O LORD, thy word is settled in heaven...

Psalm 119:148 – Mine eyes prevent the night watches, that I might...

Psalm 120:1 – In my distress I cried unto the LORD, and he heard...

Psalm 121: 1-8 – My help cometh from the LORD, which made...

Psalm 139:1, 6-8 – O LORD, thou hast searched me, and known me...

Psalm 143:8 – cause me to know the way wherein I should walk; ...

Psalm 145:2 – Everyday will I bless thee; and I will praise thy name...

Psalm 150:6 – Let everything that hath breath praise the LORD...

Praise is what we do!

Make a joyful noise unto the LORD, all ye lands. Serve the Lord with gladness: come before his presence with singing. Know ye that the LORD he is God: It is he that hath made us, and not we ourselves; we are his people, and the sheep of his pasture. Enter into his gates with thanksgiving, and into his courts with praise: be thankful unto him, and bless his name. For the LORD is good; his mercy is everlasting; and his truth endureth to all generations.

CHAPTER 21

PERMISSION TO GRIEVE

I am amazed once again at the faithfulness of God! Why do I say that? You might remember toward the beginning of the book that I mentioned that I thought Carmen should be the one to write a book on grieving, since she had so many painful experiences in this area too, over the years. Well, to my amazement as I was sorting through some of my papers the other day, I came across an article that Carmen had written back in 2007. I can't even remember her giving me a copy of it either, but suddenly—there it was!

Guess what the title on the article was? It is called, "Permission to Grieve." My mouth flew open in amazement at the faithfulness of God. She did write on grieving after all. Not only that, but as I continued to look through my papers, I found another paper which she had written for her Master of Divinity degree. Believe it or not, it is called "Victory Over Grief." All I can say is, what a mighty God we serve. He is faithful even unto death, isn't He!

Of course, I had to include some of these writings in my book (word for word), so that you can hear a little of her perspective on this powerful topic. It was written sometime during the Thanksgiving and Christmas season (as you will soon be able to see), along with a powerful acronym out of the words—permission to grieve. Here is what she said:

Permission to Grieve
By: Minister Carmen D. Murray

"Happy Thanksgiving! Merry Christmas! This is the season to be jolly! Not necessarily so. This can be a very difficult time for some of us who have experienced the loss of a loved one. As we anticipate the holiday without our loved one, it has the potential to be a time of overwhelming sadness and despair.

Some people will fight me on this reality. Especially the Christians who have not experienced the devastation of loss. They will religiously tell you things like, "Your loved one is in a better place." "All things work together for the good."

While that does provide comfort, the pain is still there. The loss must be acknowledged and addressed, both psychologically and spiritually. Besides, Jesus wept and we can as well.

I believe God gives us permission to grieve...with Hope! Just as our loving Heavenly Father gives us permission to grieve, will you give him permission to heal your broken heart? Through it all, give yourself permission to enjoy your holidays."[18]

Now here is the acronym she wrote for **Permission To Grieve:**

P   **Pray** for God to strengthen you for this season.
E   **Expect** things to be different. It is true, things are different now.
R   **Receive** God's unconditional love for you during this very sensitive time.
M   **Make** an effort to spend time with others during this time, especially when you do not feel like being bothered with others.

I   **Increase** your time in prayer and in God's Word.

S   **Share** your testimony. This is how we overcome.

S   **Seek** counseling from your local church and or professional help from a Christian therapist if necessary.

I   **Initially,** you may feel alone. God is with you.

O   **Opportune** time to volunteer your time to help others.

N   **Never** beat yourself up about things you cannot change in the relationship you had with your deceased loved one.

T   **Take** one day at a time.

O   **Open** your heart to a trusted friend. Journal writing may help as well.

G   **Get** out of your normal routine. Do something fun and relaxing.

R   **Reflect** on the positive memories.

I   **Ignite** a passion for something you have always wanted to do.

E   **Everybody** grieves differently. Don't compare yourself with others.

V   **Victory** is inevitable.

E   **Expect** God's power, presence and provision found in His Word to overwhelm you in this season.[19]

Lastly, from a portion of her Master of Divinity paper entitled **"Victory Over Grief,"** she is still expounding in this next paper on the topic permission to grieve. She writes some questions you may have for God about grieving, and then gives a loving response back from God's heart to those who are experiencing the pain of a broken heart.

"Victory Over Grief," by Minister Carmen D. Murray

She writes:

Can I cry?
Can I laugh?
Can I wonder about the future?
Can I run 'til I'm exhausted?
Can I pound on the table?
Can I scream to the top of my lungs?
Can I be mute for a while?
Can I question God?
Can I? Can I? Can I?
Yes, you can. You have my permission to grieve.
Will you give me permission to heal your broken heart?[20]

Carmen goes on to say:

>"If God can give us victory over grief, then why am I in so much pain. Jesus conquered grief and death — this conquer is in the realm of the Spirit, in our soulish realm it gets tight. God does give us permission to grieve. Yet, based on the revelation of Jesus Christ and His ability to be touched with the feelings of our infirmities, He calls us to a new level to trust Him in the area of our emotions. It is a strange dichotomy.

>On one hand, he says cry and he says wipe your weeping eyes. I'm confused. Which is it? I say both — do both. But a word of caution, do not be overtaken by overwhelming grief. Deal with grief according to the Word of God. I acknowledge my emotions and feelings, but I choose to be dominated by my spirit.

What does the Word say? "Be strong in the Lord and in the power of His might." It says, Weeping may endure for a night but joy comes in the morning, and it also says, "Greater is He that is in me than he that is in the world." [21]

Isn't that powerful! God allowed Carmen to encourage us in our process of grieving; even though she is "absent" from this realm of life. This is just another reminder of the power of leaving a legacy that I spoke of earlier in another chapter. This is a reminder of how important it is to leave something that can be a blessing to those left behind. It's also amazing that her topic of choice would be grieving! Now, from my personal perspective; that could be nobody but a mighty awesome God, who could pull off something like this! He never ceases to amaze me at His faithfulness!

CHAPTER 22

THE TRUTH ABOUT GOD

In the beginning God created the heavens and the earth...

Genesis 1:1

And ye shall know the truth, and the truth shall make you free.

John 8:32

The people who know their God will display strength and take action.

Daniel 11:32 (NASB)

I think I just may have saved the best part of this book for last in this chapter, and the next few chapters to come—just like Jesus did at the wedding feast in Cana of Galilee (John 2:1-11). That was when He performed the miracle of turning the water into wine, after all the other wine had ran out. By that, I mean He saved the best for last!

It was not my intention actually to add anything else to this book; however, the only wise God had something else in mind, and I am so glad He did! It sure is a good reminder that it pays to listen to God's voice!

I simply could not close this book without dealing with a 'major' issue as to why it is so challenging to get through the grieving process. What might that be?

It is concerning what we believe about—GOD. Because I am a defender of the faith once delivered to the saints (Jude 1:3), I must take some responsibility to do my part in releasing the truth about God, according to the scriptures. This will help us all not to fall into "error" thinking about God.

When we don't have a right concept of God, especially in the area of grieving over the passing of loved ones, we may end up drawing some seriously wrong conclusions in our minds about who God is. We just may end up like Eve did when satan (speaking through the serpent) planted a demonic idea, in a suggestive way to her, that God was being "unfair" by not allowing them to eat of the forbidden tree in the midst of the garden—that God doesn't want you to be as wise as He is. To suggest that God is "unfair," or holding out on us in some way, is an "accusation" against God's character, attributes, and His very nature.

Eve did not seem to understand that God is "holy," meaning He is so "other than" as my pastor would say; and because He is holy, so are His actions too. It would be against His nature to be unfair. From a "human wisdom" perspective, He may *seem* to be unfair when we are having some bad experiences upon the earth, but, in truth, that would be "inconsistent" with His nature.

That's one very important reason why we need to know the truth about God. Seeing God right affects how we see ourselves—in Him, and it affects how we "relate" to Him. It affects whether we can approach Him with *freedom* and *confidence,* and it affects most of all our ability to "worship" Him in Spirit and in truth (John 4:24).

We must learn what God is really like according to the truth of scripture, not according to what satan has to say about Him. Otherwise, we will end up being deceived, just like Eve was.

There are so many wonderful things to understand about God's "attributes," as we seek to know Him better. He is the God of peace and there is a peace that comes from being in His presence, that only He can give us. But, how can we rightly see Him this way if, at the same time, He seems to be a God of "confusion" in our minds, rather than a God of peace. He can't be both, can He? According to the scriptures God is *not* the author of confusion, but of peace (1 Cor. 14:33).

The bible refers to this peace (that comes from God) as a peace that passes all understanding (Phil. 4:7). This peace is so powerful that, with our natural minds, we cannot even understand or comprehend it fully! How we can have "internal peace" in the midst of all kinds of confusing circumstances and pain is absolutely amazing!

We need God's peace as a guard for our hearts and minds. His peace is "protective." It keeps us "stable" in an unstable world. It keeps us from being overwhelmed by the attacks of the enemy of our souls! Our enemy is the devil, and every demon spirit who comes to attack our minds and hearts with confusion, fear, frustration, anger and so much more. Satan is a tormentor and a deceiver, and will stop at nothing to deceive us about who this great and awesome God is that we serve!

We can easily fall into error thinking by believing what the devil has to say to us about God.

Even some unbelievers and perhaps some misguided saints, may have some negative things to say about Him, as well. That's why we must come into the knowledge of the "truth" concerning God. We must not exalt our bad earthly experiences here over who He is.

We must tap into two of the most powerful ways in which God reveals Himself to us, which are through His Word and by His Spirit. Not to mention how God reveals Himself through His created order in the universe, which leaves everyone without excuse for knowing that He exists (Rom. 1:1). Also, everyone will be without excuse for understanding that He is real, and that He is a loving God who loves all those whom He has created! However, as my pastor says so well, *"He loves us just the way we are, but He loves us too much to leave us that way!"*

For sure, none of us really know God—perfectly! We will still be learning about this only wise, Sovereign God that we serve throughout eternity! However (thank God), because of His faithfulness in preserving the scriptures (over all this time), we have the benefit of knowing Him to some degree. This is because He wants to be *known.* All of this being said, we still must admit that we only know Him in part. Yet there remains so much more to be known about Him, if we seek to be intimately acquainted with Him and know His heart for all people. But we don't just want to know *about* Him, we want to "know Him" in truth, in a very personal and relational way!

Sometimes when you don't know someone very well (naturally speaking), you can easily come to the wrong conclusion about them. You may think that they are guilty of some things that they actually are not. You may even get angry and frustrated with them because you just don't understand their behavior or conduct.

You may even accuse them falsely, even though at first you may have thought of them as being a really good person. However, one day they may do something that seems out of character, or that you just don't understand, and so you may find yourself (at this point) turning against them. It happens this way sometimes because we just may not "know" them quite as well as we may have thought we did in the beginning.

It can also be the same way in our relationship and fellowship with God. We may have already accepted Him by faith through our Lord and Savior, Jesus Christ (Rom. 10:9-10). We may even be in fellowship with Him as well. However, we still may find ourselves listening to the voice of the enemy about who God really is, since the devil really does have a voice too (Psalm 55:3).

We may be deceived into listening to his voice rather than God's. Satan has a lot to say against God, in order to come between us and Him relationally, since God is a relational God. Could satan be after your "relationship" and "fellowship" with God when he speaks to you? What might be his intention?

Could it be that satan is somewhat of a master at seeking to separate us from God? According to the apostle Paul, in Romans 8:35-38, that is exactly what he is trying to do on a regular basis. But what is satan seeking to separate us from, specifically? In this text, Paul tells us that he is seeking to separate us from the "love of God" which is in Christ Jesus.

In other words, the highest expression of the love that God has for us was manifested in Jesus Christ. God sent His only one-of-a-kind Son into the world to die for our sins, because of His "love" for us (John 3:16). So, what better plan or strategy of attack against God and our love relationship with Him, than to bring into question His love for us?

God united us through Jesus Christ, and now the devil, in his anger against God, seeks to separate what God has already joined together—in Christ.

Since the love of God is in Christ, then we need to assume the same posture or attitude that we see in the apostle Paul in Romans 8. Here is what he said:

> "Who shall separate us from the love of Christ? Shall tribulation, or distress, or persecution, or famine, or nakedness, or peril, or sword? As it is written, for thy sake we are killed all the day long; we are accounted as sheep for the slaughter. Nay, in all these things we are more than conquerors through him that loved us."

Listen to what the apostle Paul goes on to say in verse 38.

> "For I am persuaded that neither death, nor life, nor angels, or principalities, nor powers, nor things present, nor things to come. Nor height, nor depth, nor any other creature, shall be able to separate us from the love of God which is in Christ Jesus our Lord."

This is our same position as believers in Jesus Christ. We have resolved (from the depth of our spiritual connection with God through Jesus Christ) that nothing shall separate us from the love of God—that is in Christ Jesus!

Not even the experience of trials, tribulation, persecution, or even death (our own death nor anybody else's) is going to separate us from Him—even when things happen that we don't understand from a human perspective. Nothing, no nothing at all, will separate us from God and His love! You need to "serve" the devil some notice right here with me, that nothing shall separate you either. Tell that liar that it won't work!

I remember telling you something in an earlier section of this book that none of us can ever afford to forget: it's the biblical truth that satan is a *liar* and, actually, according to the scriptures, he is the father of lies (John 8:44). This should mean to us, as believers, that we cannot *trust* anything he has to say to us about God or anything else. After all, if you knew somebody was a liar (in this natural realm), then why would you be listening to them? That's a good question to think about, isn't it!

Satan is a liar and a divider of all healthy relationships, whether those relationships are between God and us, the family, or between us as believers in the family of God. These are all "vital relationships" that he would love to "disconnect" us from. That's why he is always lying and trying to divide! This is one of his major weapons in his toolbox.

Satan uses these tactics to create doubts about the faithfulness of God, which can negatively affect our faith and confidence in Him. He plants seeds of distrust in our minds against God. When we are in a state of grieving, believe me, God's enemy and ours will have plenty to say about Him to us.

After all, satan did talk to Jesus during his wilderness temptation, didn't he?

In Matthew 4:9 it says:

> **"And [the devil] saith unto him, All these things will I give thee, if thou wilt fall down and worship me."**

Then in Matthew 4:10, it says:

> **"Then saith Jesus unto him, Get thee hence, Satan: for it is written, Thou shalt worship the Lord thy God, and him only shalt thou serve."**

I am just making the point here that the devil does have a voice, but, thank God, so do we! We should have something to say back to him about what he says to us that is *not* in harmony with the scriptures, just like Jesus did. We should have a good *"it is written"* to hit him back with—immediately! Nothing but the power of the Word of God, launched out of your mouth, can *effectively* do that! That's another reason that it is so important to memorize and meditate on the scriptures until they become more than just "head" knowledge but rather, "heart" knowledge!" Then you can speak them out with confidence and authority!

So, what type of things might the devil be saying to us about God, you might be wondering? I think this would be a good place to bring in some thoughts from Neil T. Anderson and Rich Miller's powerful book, *Walking in Freedom.* I think he says it best, so I will share with you a few of the things he said concerning what may come up in our mind about God.

He is not addressing grieving specifically in these statements, but rather dealing with some of the wrong belief systems you may have toward God. So, I know this will be helpful to you on your journey to know our Father God in a greater way. It will also arm you with the "truth" about God as you stand against those lies.

He starts by saying **"I renounce the lie that my Father God is:**

1. Distant and disinterested
2. Insensitive and uncaring
3. Stern and demanding
4. Passive and cold
5. Absent or too busy for me
6. Never satisfied with what I do; impatient or angry
7. Mean, cruel or abusive
8. Trying to take all the fun out of life
9. Controlling or manipulative
10. Condemning or unforgiving
11. Nit-picking, exacting or perfectionistic[22]

Then he goes on to say some "truth" statements about our Father God across from the lies about God, along with added scripture references. I am unable to list all that he is saying in his excellent (side by side) format presentation, but I hope you will still get the point. He says these things under the title, **I joyfully accept the truth that my Father God is**:

"Intimate and involved, kind and compassionate, accepting and filled with joy and love, warm and affectionate, always with me and eager to be with me, patient and slow to anger, loving, gentle and protective, trustworthy, and He wants to give me a full life; His will is good, acceptable and perfect for me, full of grace and mercy, and he gives me freedom to fail, tenderhearted, forgiving; His heart and arms are always open to me, committed to my growth and proud of me as His growing child."[23]

After reading all of this, it just might be a good idea (if you found yourself believing some of those lies I listed) to do some "renouncing," as Neil Anderson encourages us to do. In my own words of explanation, the term "renouncing" has to do with breaking allegiances with, breaking ties or loyalty with a belief system.

So, if you have had some wrong belief systems about God, your heavenly Father, don't feel too bad about that, because you certainly are not alone! Please don't go on a guilt trip because that would not be the will of God; just take time to *renounce* them, and *embrace* the truth about God.

He loves us, He cares for us as the ultimate Father, and He is always concerned about what concerns you and I. He knows your pain and your sorrow. He actually carried them in His own body on a tree, called the cross (Isaiah 53)! He is your friend for the journey and He will never leave you or forsake you. He will never relax His hold upon you. Hebrews 13:5-6 (AMP).

I still must hasten on to ask you to remember this, however, that even in His love He will still allow some things to happen—that we may not always understand—for a higher purpose than we can comprehend in our humanity.

That's why the bible says his ways are higher than our ways and his thoughts are too (Isaiah 55:9). That's also why I said to you before, that you will have to learn how to *trust* Him, even when you can't *trace* Him!

In the final analysis of it all, we will still have to admit that He is God and we are not, and that Father God always knows best!

As for us, perhaps we just need to say the words of the song my earthly father sang all the time when I was a young girl, "We will understand it better by and by."

Lastly, here are a few scriptures for you to meditate on that will help you get to know the truth about the Almighty God we serve much better, as the days go by:

Ps. 139:1-18; Ps. 103:8-14; Zeph. 3:17; Rom. 15:7; Isa. 40:11; Hos. 11:3,4; Jer. 31:20; Ezek. 34:11-16; Heb. 13:5; Exod. 34:6; 2 Pet. 3:9; Ps. 18:2; Isa. 42:3; Jer. 31:3; Lam. 3:22,23; John 10:10; Rom. 12:1,2; Luke 15:11-16; Heb. 4:15,16; Ps. 130:1-4; Luke 15:17-24. Rom. 8:28,29; 2 Cor. 7:4; Heb. 12:5-11.

CHAPTER 23

BITTER OR BETTER?

"But now Jesus, our High Priest, has been given a ministry that is far superior to the old priesthood, for he is the one who mediates for us a far better covenant with God, based on better promises."

Hebrew 8:6 (NLT)

"See to it that no one falls short of the grace of God and that no bitter root grows up to cause trouble and defile many."

Hebrews 12:15 (NIV)

Even though many good things have been said concerning how to gain a healthy perspective of grieving, someone may still be wondering when they will feel "better" about it all. There have been so many times when people have lost loved ones not only through sickness, but through major tragedies like car accidents, plane crashes, accidents on the job, even murder and suicide too. Most of the time, sudden deaths like these are even more difficult to overcome than a long illness that we knew could possibly lead to death. These type of transitions are far more difficult to overcome, as you seek to come into the place where you actually begin to feel—better.

That's why I wanted to address the very real intense pain of it all from an emotional perspective. I just want to say this to those of you who are still in so much pain and agony from the experience of it all.

It may have been many years ago since your loved one passed on, but you still find yourself desperately struggling to feel better.

Let me share with you the difference in where you are right now and where you really want to be. It's called *submitting* to the process. Some people quit before they get all the way through the process. By that I mean some have been unable to cry about it all, to express their frustration, to be angry, or even to express feelings of being afraid. They are trying their best to face what feels like a very uncertain future, in the absence of their loved one.

Some people have never talked to anyone about how they feel. Holding it all within yourself will only devastate you that much more. Those emotions have to go somewhere. If you choose to "stuff" them, they will just crop up somewhere else when you least expect it, and that could end up exploding on someone else.

Some people just try to go on with life, without acknowledging the pain of it all, which can hold you back from getting better. Therefore, I want to encourage you to acknowledge the pain, but don't try to live back there. You may need to have a good cry, or talk with a trusted friend, or consult good pastoral leadership. You may need to do all of these things. Whatever you decide, you must do something other than *isolate* yourself from others in dealing with your pain. Just ask God for wisdom in how you should proceed in getting help with your personal issues.

Let me share with you a little more of the grief and pain that I have experienced over the years, in the passing of many of my loved ones, so you will realize more and more that you are not alone on this journey.

I have experienced much grief in my life, not only over Carmen, but my father and mother too. I could not have asked for better parents than they were. Also, the passing of two of my brothers, Tony Roberson and Albert Roberson Jr.

My grieving experiences also extend to include two of my pastors, who I loved and served under for so many years. So, I really feel those of you who have had pastors you loved and served under, who passed on from this expression of life. That is a really tough time for the members of the church to get through; I really feel your pain! Then, there have also been countless church members I had grown close to over the years, who are now deceased. These have been some really difficult times, as well.

My mother (who was a wonderful missionary) died of congestive heart failure and other medical complications. My father (who was a minister of the gospel) died of lung cancer from many years of smoking. One of my brothers (next to me in age) was murdered by someone who "claimed" to be his friend. My oldest brother (who served in the army most of his life) had a heart attack and died, many years later after his service in the military had ended. So, I just want you to know that I feel you!

The reality is that, in the days ahead, I will sooner or later experience the passing of many others (if I live on in this expression of life as I hope to), that is, unless Jesus decides to return in my lifetime, which would be absolutely awesome! Either way, it has been quite a journey getting through the passing of each of these loved ones! I have actually been to more funerals of loved ones and other believers than I can count!

At Carmen's funeral, I cannot tell you how sad and empty I felt inside, as I told you before. Looking at the physical temple she once lived in was overwhelming to say the least. I was in so much intense pain that I felt like it would last a lifetime.

However, when I look at myself today (now that some years have passed since she went home), I think to myself—what a mighty God we serve. He has amazed me once again at His amazing grace! I can honestly say that I feel so much *better*! How much better, you might be wondering? Better enough to have written this book to you, for the glory of God. Better enough to have went back to school to get a college degree. Better enough to continue serving in my church home, to be a blessing to my church family by teaching and sharing the good news of Jesus Christ with the lost, and so much more.

Yes, I am so much "better" and you will be too, if you *submit* yourself to the process. Let God heal you of your broken heart, so you can go on to make a difference in the life of someone else, just as I am now doing by His grace. I am confident that you can do it through Christ who strengthens you (Phil. 4:13).

Besides all of this, I know that Carmen would not want me to feel the same way I felt back then at her funeral. She would want me to be so much better! I knew her well enough to know that. She would be so upset with me if I did anything less. One thing I knew only too well about Carmen, is that she loved and enjoyed life! She understood that Jesus came to give us life, and that more abundantly (John 10:10). She was so full of the joy of the Lord, and she knew how to make every single day count for His glory.

She was a mighty woman of influence in the earth. One time, she was told by one of our former pastors that she would be like E. F. Hutton; when she spoke, people would—listen. I can sure witness to that, and many others who knew her can too! She was always moving on by faith in the one true and living God. She did not get stuck in the painful experiences of her life. By God's grace, she kept on getting—better.

Even though I am absolutely certain that what I am about to say to you in the closing of this chapter will not apply to everyone who might read this book, I still feel compelled to ask a closing question for those who might be struggling with intense pain—and sincerely want to get better. I don't want to close this chapter without asking you what may seem like a very strange question to ask. Just remember that I am asking it out of love and concern for you and your spiritual and "emotional health" in Christ. Believe me, my motives are pure; I really have your best interest at heart!

Before I ask you this question, I want to soften the blow of it by telling you that Jesus did the same thing in a story in the Bible. He asked a man He encountered, the same "strange" question. In John 5:1-15, there was a man who had been lying by the pool of Bethesda for 38 years needing a healing. Other disabled folks were lying around this area of the pool too.

They were believing that they would be healed when the angel would come down to stir the waters of the pool. That's when Jesus came along and asked this particular man a very strange question. He said to the man, *"Do you want to get well?"* It is somewhat of a strange question to ask of someone you saw was sick, I think. It seems natural to believe that if someone was sick, then they would automatically want to get well, right?

This man's issue was physical to some degree it seems, but not without some rather serious spiritual implications hiding behind it. You can tell this by the way the man answered Jesus' question. He responded, *"While I am trying to get in, someone else goes down ahead of me."* The truth is that not being able to get into the water was not the main issue, as other preachers have pointed out over the years from this text.

In 38 years, he could have rolled, scooted, and done so many other things (in faith) to get into that pool over this long period of time. No, that was not the real problem. It was more about his mentality or mindset. You see, after Jesus heard the man's response, in His mercy He healed him instantly, and he was able to pick up his mat and walk after all that time—once he obeyed Jesus' command by faith. Jesus broke him out of his bag of "excuses" and "self-imposed limitations" about why he couldn't get well. His greatest need was for Jesus the healer, and to believe by faith that he could be healed, whether he got into the pool or not. Any time Jesus shows up in our situation, anything can happen!

Do you Want to Get Well?

That's why I am asking you this same question, *"Do you want to get well?"* Jesus is the one who can heal you everywhere you hurt. He can touch you in places that no one else can.

There have been so many times in all of our lives, I am sure, that God has provided some extensions of help for us from outside resources. What I mean is, using the hands of his people, according to their gifts and callings, in order to help us along the journey.

However, we must always keep looking to Jesus, who is our healer. He cannot only heal us, but He has the power to make us—whole! He is full of compassion for the condition of His people (Psalm 145:8; Ecc. 2:11).

We must not fall into self-pity, or even make excuses for why we cannot move forward by faith. We must not get stuck in our pain and sorrow. A better solution would be to acknowledge our pain to the Lord, and get His "wisdom" on what we need to do to keep moving through the grieving process.

The Bible says that, "Christ has been made unto us, wisdom, righteousness, sanctification, and redemption" (1 Cor. 1:30). Therefore, since Christ has been made unto us wisdom, then He will guide us into all truth by His Spirit (John 16:13). Remember, "self-pity" keeps our focus on ourselves, and not on the one who can make us so much—better! Trust me, it really is going to get better. It may be a short time, or it may be a few years from now before you *fully* experience it, but one day you will look back and say, Wow! Thank you, Lord, I see what you mean. I feel so much better!

After You Have Suffered a While

The Bible says in I Peter 5:10,

"but after you have suffered a while may the God of all grace, who hath called us into His eternal glory by Christ Jesus, make you perfect, establish, strengthen, settle you."

I like the way this verse is amplified in the Amplified Bible too, as we seek more understanding about this issue of getting better after we have suffered a while. It says:

> **"After you have suffered for a little while, the God of all grace [who imparts His blessing and favor] who called you to His own eternal glory in Christ, will Himself complete, confirm, strengthen, and establish you [making you what you ought to be]."**

I can almost hear somebody asking this question after reading this text, "How long is a while?" I wish I could tell you, but only God knows the answer to that! However, I assure you that He won't let it last too long! He knows just how much we can bear. Rest assured, that after suffering you will be strengthened and established in the faith, and so much more.

As much as we don't want to suffer, there are some good things that can come out of it. You will be "better" for having endured the process of grieving. You will become "stable" and stronger if you *choose* to handle it right. Not only that, but you will be able to help others through the process out of the stability you have found in Him. I assure you that God won't let the suffering last too long.

Here is a good key to help you get through the suffering in a glorious way. It's all going to come down to the power of a—choice! You are going to need to choose to *focus* on the outcome rather than the *suffering,* just like Jesus did. How did He endure all that suffering at the cross? If we look at Jesus' perspective of suffering and where His focus was, I think we will get a good clue. In Hebrews 12:2 it says:

> **"Looking unto Jesus, the author and finisher of our faith, who for the joy that was set before Him endured the cross, despising the shame, and is set down at the right hand of the throne of God."**

Here is how this same verse reads in the Amplified Bible:

> "[Looking away from all that will distract us and] focusing our eyes on Jesus, who is the Author and Perfecter of faith [the first incentive for our belief and the One who brings our faith to maturity], who for the joy [of accomplishing the goal] set before Him endured the cross, disregarding the shame, and sat down at the right hand of the throne of God [revealing His deity, His authority, and the completion of His work]."

Jesus "focused" on the joy that was yet to come. What was that joy? It was the joy of the many sons and daughters of righteousness who would come forth out of it all. He focused on the fruit, i.e., the harvest of souls, rather than the pain of it all.

This must be our same approach. He told us to keep looking unto Him as the example of this kind of "perspective" of suffering, and then we will be able to experience that same joy too. You will be so much better when you get on the other side of through! It is always your choice to be bitter or better. Which one will you choose?

A Root of Bitterness

> "See to it that no one comes short of the grace of God; that no root of bitterness spring up causes trouble, and by it, many be defiled."

> **Hebrews 12:15 (NASB)**

199

> **"Look after each other so that none of you fails to receive the grace of God. Watch out that no poisonous root of bitterness grows up to trouble you, corrupting many."**
>
> **Hebrews 12:15 (NLT)**

Once something gets "rooted," it is so much harder to dig up, but if we deal with it before the "root formation" takes place, then we will end up in a healthy place! You can tell the "signs" and "symptoms" of when you are becoming bitter by listening to the words that come out of your mouth.

The bible tells us that it is out of the abundance of our hearts that the mouth speaks (Luke 6:45b). What we really believe gets expressed out of our mouths. Our "words" reveal what is in our hearts, whether it is good or bad! The heart is the soil that bitterness grows in if we let it, then at some point it overflows out of our mouths. This bitterness not only has the potential to defile us, but others around us as well, according to the Word of God.

So, having understood this truth (after all is said and done), just remember that it is a "decision" that you have the power to make, by God's amazing grace; not to be bitter because of your life experiences. I am so confident that you will make the right choice!

CHAPTER 24

All for the Glory of God

"You are worthy, O Lord, to receive glory and honour and power: for thou hast created all things, and for thy pleasure they are and were created."

Revelation 4:11

For everything comes from him and exists by his power and is intended for his glory. All glory to him forever! Amen.

Romans 11:36

"I have brought you glory on earth by finishing the work you gave me to do."

John 17:4

Isn't it amazing, that when Jesus was about to leave this earth realm, His mind was focused on having given God the glory through the life He had lived upon the earth. This is what Jesus is saying in John 17:4, which is His high priestly prayer, as He is about to return to the Father. He lived His life with a powerful sense of purpose and meaning. He had His focus on having a specific assignment in the earth, and a mind to *finish* it for the glory of God.

When all is said and done, the real question for us will be, did our lives in the earth bring any glory to God? That's what is really important. It's not so much how long we lived, but did our life leave an "impact" on anybody else's life. Did we live in such a way in the earth that it brought glory to His name?

This is the mindset that God wants all of us to have, who are still living in this expression of life. He wants us to live a life that pleases Him, since that is actually why we were created (Rev. 4:11). The term "glory" or "glorify," used in relation to God in simple terms, means to bring "pleasure to." It means to bring honor to His name, to live your earthly life in such a way that it points back to Him, when people see how you lived your life before God. Like it says in Matthew 5:16,

> **"Let your light so shine before men, so that they may see your good works and glorify your Father which is in heaven."**

It's not about being busy doing a lot of things, but rather "modeling" like Jesus did the life that pleases God. It's how you live from day to day at home, in the workplace, at the beauty shop, in the grocery store, and so on. It is your "character" that is on display in how you treat people as you go through the journey of life.

It is the fruit that the Spirit produces in you and through you, so that you can display His glory in the earth. It is "love, joy, peace, forbearance, kindness, goodness, faithfulness, gentleness and self-control" (Gal. 5:22-23). It is like the character of Christ alive in you and me that helps us to treat others with love, respect, dignity, and honor.

It is to treat people with a spirit of "kindness" that flows out of us toward others. It makes them wonder what is it about us that makes us this way. It speaks to them, even when we may not have said a word out of our mouths. It "grabs" their attention and it causes others to want to listen to what we have to say. As my pastor always says, *"The model precedes the message."*

They will hunger for what we have when we can get our minds off of ourselves long enough to impact someone else's life for the glory of God.

Our lives were designed to make a "healthy impact" on the lives of others. God does not only want us to know Him, He also expects that we will make Him known to others throughout the earth. God loves people from *"every tribe, language, people, and nation"* Rev. 5:9 (NIV). His heart is for the nations! He wants people from every "ethnic group" to know Him. Since He loves them, then we should too.

I hope I don't shock your system too much in saying this, but even those who have proven to be His enemies and those who are unjust and evil are included in His love. His offer of salvation is for "all" mankind! He wants them also to have a *chance* to be saved. He wants them to know that He is the one true and living God and that there is no other besides Him.

God wants them to know that He wrapped Himself in human flesh, and that He came down to earth and died for their sins. He is not willing that any should perish but that all should come to repentance (2 Pet. 3:9). He wants them to have a change of mind and heart, and then He wants to use them for his glory too!

People are in pain everywhere throughout the earth, not just believers but "nonbelievers" as well. Pain knows no nationality. It impacts every culture, every people, every group—globally. No one is exempt from pain. They need hope and answers that can only be found through God and His Word. They want to know if God really exists, and does He care about them and their plight in life—just like the people of Aleppo in Syria who are suffering terribly, as one of many examples.

They need to know that we as believer's in Jesus Christ care about them, and are praying for them too.

We must remember as the body of Christ that Jesus did not build "walls" between people, He built a "bridge" that allows *all* people who believe in Him as Lord to crossover through the blood of His cross! It says so in the bible, in Ephesians 2:14, 15 (NLT), which reads like this:

> **"For Christ himself has brought peace to us. He united Jews and Gentiles into one people when, in his own body on the cross, he broke down the wall of hostility that separated us.**
>
> **He did this by ending the system of law with its commandments and regulations. He made peace between Jews and Gentiles by creating in himself one new people from the two groups.**
>
> **Together as one body, Christ reconciled both groups to God by means of his death on the cross, and our hostility toward each other was put to death."**

In the world's system or their way of doing things; they may build walls, but that is not how we do it in the Kingdom, i.e., under the government of God. We lead people to the one who bridged the gap, so they can be forgiven of their sins and cross over into the Kingdom of God, thereby becoming a new person in Christ Jesus (2 Cor. 5:17). Now, that is what you call "the good news of the gospel!

We as believers have the good news of the gospel that they have been waiting for, for far too long. So, do not allow yourself to grieve too long.

There are people waiting on us to "arise" and "shine" and glorify God in the earth (Isa. 60:1-3). They need to see our "strength" in God, and how He is able to see us through any situation or circumstance. They need to hear our testimony of how He brought us out when we put our trust in Him. They need to know that He is faithful and will be their guide too, even unto the end; if they put their trust in Him (Ps. 48:14 (NIV)).

Perhaps, as you read this chapter, you may feel that you have not done very much up to this point that brings glory to God. Please don't be discouraged about that. We have certainly all made our mistakes in life, so you are not alone. However, please think of it this way: you are still here, so you still have an opportunity to make an impact in the earth.

Remember, God is patient, longsuffering, and merciful! He is still holding your soul in life, so there is still time (Ps. 66:8,9). Just repent, which is to have another mind (after consideration and regret). Then don't procrastinate! Get up, dust yourself off, get out of those "mourning" clothes and arise and shine for His glory. You still have something to give to a dying world!

I think we probably could all take a powerful lesson from King David on arising and shinning after the death of a loved one. He was believing God to save his child's life after he had sinned with Bathsheba and gotten her pregnant. Then, if that was not bad enough, he went on to have her husband Uriah killed by having him put on the front line in battle. He then went on to take Uriah's wife (Bathsheba) for himself (see 2 Sam., 11th chapter).

Bathsheba gave birth to the child, but then the child became sick.

David was fasting and praying for the child's life to be spared, after the baby had been struck with sickness that was unto death, although he didn't know it at the time. This situation put him in a really bad space. In fact, he was in such a bad state that he went into his house and laid on the ground and refused to eat.

The elders of his family tried to pull him up from the ground but could not. However, once he got word that the child died (as painful as this had to be), he then accepted the child's death to the amazement of them all. The servants were afraid to let him know that the baby had died. They were afraid that he would do something terrible (perhaps to himself) in response if he knew the truth about the child.

However, much to their surprise, when he saw them whispering he realized that the baby must be dead; and so he asked them outright if the baby was dead. They told him yes. So, he got up off the floor and even cleaned himself up and ate food. David said to his servants, when they asked him about his very unusual behavior, considering the situation he found himself in:

> **"While the baby was still alive, I fasted, and I cried. I thought, "Who knows? Maybe the LORD will feel sorry for me and let the baby live. But now that the baby is dead, why should I fast? Someday I will go to him, but he cannot come back to me."**
>
> 2 Samuel 12:21-22

Then the text goes on to say:

> **"Then David comforted Bathsheba his wife."**
>
> Vs. 24

You see, David knew that this part of his life with his child was now over, and he could not change the outcome no matter what he did at this point. So, he went in to be with his wife again and she conceived and had another child, a son, and David named him Solomon. He made the necessary "adjustment" out of the strength of his relationship with God. Was it easy? I think we all know the answer to that. No, it must have been one of the most challenging times of his life.

To lose a baby has to be absolutely devastating. Talk about a broken heart! However, the truth is life must go on. How will you do it? It happens when you choose to give God your pain, and trust him to give you back the courage to "believe" again. To believe what, you might be thinking? To be able to believe that there is still a hope a future for you and your family or whatever you have left, in the days to come. Believing that God still has a plan and he will work it out after the counsel of his own will (Eph. 1:11). I think it is the power of making a firm "decision," and it is a choice we all have to make at some point in our lives. I am believing God that you will make the right one, and I know ultimately that you will be so glad you did!

CHAPTER 25

God Will Take Care of You

"He that spared not his own Son but gave him up for us all, won't he also give us everything else?"
Romans 8:32(NLT)

"Cast all your anxiety on him because he cares for you."
I Peter 5:7

I will not leave you as orphans; I will come to you.
John 14:18

"Elisha said to her, "What shall I do for you? Tell me, what do you have in the house?" And she said, your servant has nothing at all she said, except a small jar of olive oil."
2 Kings 4:2

After the passing of loved ones, we may become consumed with fears and worries about how our personal needs are going to be met. You see, having people in our lives helps to "fulfill" all kinds of needs we have. Some of these needs are emotional, physical, mental, and financial too. This is just a reality of life. If you were married, then there will be a loss of companionship and (let's be real by including) physical needs too. All of these are legitimate needs.

Now, what about when a father dies? If a father in the family dies, then this may have so many diverse impacts on his family, since he was created to be the head of the family. He was the priest of his household.

It could impact how the children view God as their heavenly Father, because they would have lost the model of fatherhood they once had, which is a very powerful role on so many levels.

A strong sense of support, love, direction, and security, is also a part of what fathers provide as well. Sometimes the men of your church may be able to help in this area, but please be led of the Lord in who you trust with your "precious" little ones too. It will also have a financial impact upon the rest of the family left here, in his absence, among other things. Even if (from your perspective) he wasn't the greatest model of a father, he was still their father.

What about when a mother dies? If a mother dies, then there will be a loss of some of the *nurturing* aspects that she as a woman may have brought to the family. Most mothers wear so many different hats in the family. I think they are just built like that by God. They are pretty good at multitasking to meet the needs of a husband and children, and very often keeping up with the cooking and cleaning too, in many cases.

It is a powerful role and everyone in the family will feel the effects of her absence. If there were children with one or both of the parents now gone, then there will be a loss on so many different levels for them. They still have to be clothed, fed, attend school, and they will have many emotional needs as well. Many grandparents are even raising their grandchildren more and more these days. Often this happens because of the loss of their father, mother or both parents!

The truth is that everyone's life is going to be impacted in some way for sure. We all play a different role in the lives of others, so something will be missing now that they are gone. Who will fulfill these many role's that surface on a daily basis?

Since we all still have to live after someone dies, these needs of ours will still have to be "fulfilled" in some way or another. Sometimes, when we are grieving we may seek to fulfill needs in our own strength, i.e., in the flesh. We may start to search in all the wrong places, and seek out the wrong kind of people to "replace" what we have lost. Please don't be too hasty right here to fulfill your own needs. When you try to do that, you just may end up birthing out an "Ishmael" rather than an "Isaac" (the promised child). Abraham and Sarah knew about this only too well. They got ahead of God's plan and now look at the outcome.

After all this time, from way back in the bible days, we are still feeling the effects of that bad decision. It happened when Sarah, who was obviously tired of waiting on God to have a child, chose to send Hagar her handmaid in to sleep with her husband, Abraham, so that the child could be hers. Abraham consented, but we will not go there! Then, Hagar got pregnant with Ishmael. If you are not familiar with this story, it is a must read in Genesis the 16th chapter. It will serve as a good warning just in case you might be tempted to step out in your *flesh* to get your needs met during this grieving process. Please, don't do it, I beg of you! It will only lead to regret!

When we try to get ahead of the plan of God for our lives, we may do something that will have very long-range, devastating effects upon us and in the lives of others. The bible says, *"For I know that in me (that is in my flesh), dwelleth no good thing"* (Rom. 7:18). God did not create us to live according to our flesh but rather after the Spirit.

Romans 8:13 says:

For if you live according to the flesh, you will die, but if by the Spirit you put to death the misdeeds of the body, you will live."

It was never His intention for us to seek to fulfill our needs for ourselves. He always wanted us to come to Him.

Do you remember how Eve tried to do that in the book of Genesis, chapter 3, through her conversation with the serpent. She "shifted" from God will take care of you, to the idea that she could take care of her own needs. She fell to "human wisdom" in looking at the tree that was forbidden by God for them to eat from, thinking perhaps that satan, speaking through the serpent—just might be right. The tree looked good for food from her "perspective;" it could even potentially make them wise too, couldn't it? Was she thinking perhaps, *Maybe God is holding out on us by forbidding us to eat from it.*

This kind of thinking is always planted by a very real enemy for sure. He set them up for a very tragic fall that impacted us all. That was of course until God turned it all around through Jesus Christ. We all know that Adam was not innocent in this situation either, since He was the "federal head" of the entire human race!

There is so much more to this story that I cannot share now, but I just want to make the point right here that satan is still using this same strategy on us, even to this very day. He is still *slandering* God and telling lies to us about the only one true and living God. It is how he gets us to sin against God. Why should he change his strategy when it seems to still be working so very well?

We must not keep falling for this demonic strategy, which happens every time we choose to lean to our own understanding (Prov. 3:5,6). God is the one that said through the writers of scripture, *"But my God shall supply all your need according to his riches in glory by Christ Jesus* (Phil. 4:19).

My pastor always says that sometimes in order to get the content (nutrients) out of the Word of God, we need to learn how to read it more slowly. When we read too fast, we usually miss some important truths from His Word. So, let's do that with this verse; let's slow it down. This verse says, "My God" which indicates a personal relationship with Him. Then it says, "shall supply all" your needs. This indicates that nothing that we need will be left out from any aspect of our lives, since it says "all." This would mean that He has every area of our life covered.

Then it says "according to His riches in glory." So then, that would mean that what He plans to do won't be able to be met by what we have in our bank accounts, or any other resources we may have in the earth realm. Everything in this earth is a "resource," but in truth, God is our only "source!" There is a difference between the two. It will be supplied according to how rich God is, not how rich we are, thank God. The needs will be met according to His riches in glory. That sounds like our needs are going to be met from another realm, doesn't it?

Then he concluded in closing this verse by saying, these needs will be supplied "by Christ Jesus." That sounds like it's flowing through the finished work of Jesus Christ at the cross. I think this speaks of our "inheritance" we have, because we are—in Christ Jesus! Therefore, all of our *provisions* are flowing from God, out of our relationship with Christ Jesus. That's powerful isn't it! The bottom line is, that it's all been taken care of!

Every provision we need comes from Him and the truth is that since God gave up his only Son for us, how will he not also give us all things to enjoy (Rom. 8:32)? This should mean to us that God is not selfish, right? He is a giving God! He wants all of our needs to be taken care of. We must learn to stay within God's boundaries when faced with needs and desires.

So, a better approach to getting our needs met within His "boundaries" would be to tell God whatever the need is, asking in faith, which is how we live the Christian life. Then watch Him work it out after the counsel of His own will (Eph. 1:11). If He chooses to use people, then He will; but if not, He won't. Sometimes He will just choose to do it all by Himself, because He is a supernatural God! We must just purpose in our hearts to be open to His will, His way. Now, I want to give you a little brief example of God using other people, after we go to Him with our needs or desires—first.

My friend Carmen never married, but she did desire to marry someday, sooner than later. So, one day she mentioned to me that she told God that she wanted to be given some flowers—you know, like you would get from a man who was your boyfriend or your husband on a special occasion.

So, she said that one day (after that time of making her request known unto Him), she was in a store buying a few things she needed. There was a man standing in front of her who was paying for his items too. He bought some flowers, and then turned around in the line and gave them to her, as she stood there in absolute amazement! She didn't even know this man. She had never seen him before in her life.

Now that might sound like a small thing to you, but that was God letting her know that He heard her request. He was meeting a need or desire in her heart, that she had at the time. He is so amazing like that! She was so excited when she told me about it and I got excited too.

What a reminder, that God would say to her in so many words, I told you I would supply *all* your need. It may not have been the way she was expecting it to happen, but it still happened! That's just one way of how God uses people to bless our lives and fulfill a need we may have. At other times, He may choose to do it all by Himself, as I said before, since He is just that powerful and He is just that kind of friend for the journey!

When Jesus was about to go to the cross, He supplied a need in His own mother's life. He made provision for her to be taken care of since he would no longer be able to, in this mother-son type of relationship. He said *"woman behold thy son,* then he said to the disciple, *"son behold your mother."* And then it goes on to say, *"and from that hour that disciple took her into his own home* (John 19:26). He was speaking to John and His very own Mother, Mary. John was being given the responsibility by Jesus to take care of His mother, in His earthly absence.

Jesus was going to the cross to die for the sins of the whole world, but He still took time to make provision for his mother. That's God once again revealing himself as a provider. So, don't get nervous, for He will provide!

Sometimes it seems like we are a lot like the disciples in a boat during a storm, when it comes to believing that God will take care of us.

During times like these we feel like saying to God,

Lord, don't you care that I am perishing? Don't you see what a mess this has left my life in? Don't you care at all? I am about to drown in this boat. I know you can't be sleeping at a time like this in my life, could you?

I know this is how you might feel, but this is not true. Let me tell you from experience that God has always been taking care of you and I from the womb even until now, in more ways than we can even imagine. In His faithfulness, He will continue to take care of us. As the old folks use to say, *"through dangers seen and unseen."* Surely, His goodness and His mercy has been following us every single day of our lives!

I am telling you the truth, that there has not been a need that I have had, since Carmen passed, that God has not met in one way or another. God is not sleeping on the job, because *"He neither slumbers or sleeps,"* (Psalm 121:4). He is always ready and available to come and see about you and I!

When the disciples were in that boat and the winds and the waves were beating against it (with the disciples in the midst of it all), Jesus got up and spoke to the winds and the waves, and He said *"peace, be still."* Then the waves and the winds obeyed Him! Yes, He cares for you and don't you ever doubt it for another moment. As the old folks use to say, *"He may not come when you want Him, but He will be right on time!"*

Don't Worry — He Will Take Care of You!

"Be anxious for nothing but in everything by prayer and supplication, let your requests be made known to God; and the peace of God,

which surpasses all understanding, will guard your hearts and minds through Christ Jesus."

Philippians 4:6-7

Since God is taking care of birds of the air and lilies of the field, surely He can and will take care of you!

> "That is why I tell you not to worry about everyday life—whether you have enough food and drink, or enough clothes to wear. Isn't life more than food, and your body more than clothing?

> Look at the birds. They don't plant or harvest or store food in barns, for your heavenly Father feeds them. And aren't you far more valuable to him than they are? Can all your worries add a single moment to your life?"

> And why worry about your clothing? Look at the lilies of the field and how they grow. They don't work or make their clothing, yet Solomon in all his glory was not dressed as beautifully as they are. And if God cares so wonderfully for wildflowers that are here today and thrown into the fire tomorrow, he will certainly care for you. Why do you have so little faith?

> So don't worry about these things saying, What will we eat? What will we drink? What will we wear? These things dominate the thoughts of unbelievers, but your heavenly Father already knows all your needs.

Don't Worry About Tomorrow:

217

Seek the kingdom of God above all else, and live righteously, and he will give you everything you need. So, don't worry about tomorrow, for tomorrow will bring its own worries. Today's trouble is enough for today."

Matthew 6:25-34

AUTHOR'S AFTERWORD

Food for Thought

As I was focusing on the writing of this book and had begun to reflect on Carmen's life, I began to wonder if perhaps our "focus" is a little misguided, concerning our temporary life on earth. What I mean is, which one should carry the most weight, the "quantity" or the "quality" of life, for us as believers in Jesus Christ? What should the emphasis be on for us?

Would it be more important (in the grand scheme of things) how *long* we live, or how *well* we live? Perhaps some of you are thinking both, and in one sense I totally agree with you. But, from another perspective, I think we should be willing to consider for a moment balancing it all out, by putting a little more emphasis on the *quality*, as we journey on toward Christlikeness.

In the society in which we currently live, the focus seems to be leaning too much toward "longevity" at times, without a clear emphasis on a "defined" purpose for living from day to day. The appeal of this fallen world seems to be focused on preserving life to get all you "can" get out of it, and then "can" all you get. It's very self-centered and self-serving, which is a product of the original "fall" of mankind, for sure.

There seems to be a desire to live a very long life, so you can do what *you* want to do. Life seems to pretty much consist of what could be called an eat, drink, and be merry type of mentality and lifestyle. It is a "worldview" that I think is clearly not in harmony with the scriptures. In many ways, it's just like in Noah's day when the Lord destroyed the earth by a flood (Genesis, 6 chapter).

The focus was not on living with a "divine purpose" and plan that their Creator had in mind for their lives. No, it seems that it was all about what they wanted, not what He wanted for their lives. Noah was out there preaching all those years that it was going to rain. But the people went right on living that kind of eat, drink and be merry lifestyle—at least until the rain actually came, just as he had said!

While I am not saying that it is wrong to have fun, enjoy life, and live a long life, I am challenging our "focus" as believers on how we use the time God has allotted to us all, since the bible does tell us our times are in his hands (Psalm 31:15). We seem to have forgotten that we are "temporary residents" here in this earth realm. In Peter 1:17b in the Amplified version of the bible, it says, "You should conduct yourselves with true reverence throughout the time of your temporary residence [on the earth, whether long or short].

That's why I think we need to find a "healthy balance" on this issue of "quantity" and "quality," because in this verse, it is saying whether our time here is long or short." Either way, we are still temporary residences. Since we are not "home" yet, then we need to start acting more like it and make the most of the time we have here, whether long or short! We need to focus more on being productive, fruitful and focused on our "dominion assignment" while we are still here.

For example, concerning the topic of death like we have been talking about in detail in this book, sometimes people say when their loved ones pass on, (especially if they passed early from our perspective),

"It's too sad, they were so young, she was only 20, or 30, or 40 years old.

She hasn't even had a chance to live a good life and enjoy it yet. It's a shame."

In the manner in which they seem to express these words at times, you can hear a little sense of *defeat* in their tone of voice. From one perspective, they may feel somehow that the devil got one up on their loved one because they died so early. Although the manner in which they died may feel like a defeat, this is really not the case. We know that the truth is that they just passed from death to life with Christ, if they were a Christian. Whether they were young, middle aged, or senior citizens, nothing will never change that. It does not get any better than that, does it? Not to mention if it was a life well lived!

A Life Well Lived

Perhaps the problem with our "perspective" of life on earth is our understanding of what it means to live "well," from a biblical perspective. Let's take a look at Jesus' life on earth as a "model" of a life lived very well, in a very short time frame. Jesus' life was very short indeed—but look how well he lived it out in the earth realm!

If someone died around 33 years old in this day and time, we would be saying, Wow! They died so early. However, within that time frame, Jesus trained twelve disciples to carry on his earthly ministry. He preached all over the known world traveling mostly by foot, other times by boat or on an animal. Either way it was a slow time-consuming transportation system in those days. Certainly, there were no cars or airplanes as modes of travel like we have today! Yet he still managed to get the job done! Jesus taught multitudes of people at one time, and still had time to be compassionate in ministering to their felt needs for food and rest.

In between times, Jesus also ministered to individuals, not to mention the miracles he performed—bodily healings and raising the dead. He ate with publicans and sinners. He exercised authority over demon spirits as they sought to block His mission on earth. Would you believe that, in the midst of all this, He still found time to commune with His Father all along the journey of life?

He was in constant touch with His Father communing and fellowshipping with Him, day by day. He challenged unholy lifestyles of people He came in contact with, to bring them into a whole new way of living.

Jesus was constantly moved with *compassion* for the marginalized, which consisted of people who were living on the edge and being unjustly treated by the cruel society in which they lived. You see, life for Jesus was all about *people* and ministering the God-kind of life to them. He was willing to use His time, energy, and all His resources toward that cause.

He was the Son of God and the Son of man, on a mission called the business of the Father. He said himself, *"I must be about my Father's Business* (Luke 2:49)."* He also told the Father *"I have finished the work thou gavest me to do* (John 17:4)."* He was focused and spent His time well by living it for the glory of God. In fact, Jesus accomplished so much in His short time on earth that the scriptures say, in John 21:25:

> **"And there are also many other things which Jesus did, the which, if they should be written every one, I suppose that even the world itself could not contain the books that should be written. Amen."**

Wow! That's awesome! That's what you call a life well lived! Perhaps at this point someone may be thinking, but that was Jesus, that's why He could accomplish so much in such a short time. That would seem like a "good excuse," except for the fact that Jesus was living within the confines of human flesh, as He walked upon the earth. He was the model for all of us of what the life that pleases God looks like, so we could follow after Him. Rev. 4:11 reveals to us that we have the same assignment, because we too were created to please God.

We were all created to glorify Him as I just spoke of in the previous chapter! In Jesus' humanity, He had human limitations, just like we do. He had a human body, so therefore He needed to eat, sleep, and do natural things just as we do. He got tired and had to rest just like us. However, in spite of these physical limitations, He still fulfilled His Father's will. He was an obedient servant and He focused on His purpose for being here.

We are followers of Christ and have the same "authority" and "power" that He invested in us by the Holy Spirit, to fulfill our Father's will too (Rom. 8:9-11). In fact, the scriptures tell us that the same power that raised Jesus from the dead is living in us.

We have a certain time frame to accomplish some mighty things in the earth for the glory of God, just as Carmen did by the grace of God. The thing is, though, that we don't know how much time we have left to accomplish it; we only know how much time we have already spent. This means that we should be asking God to teach us to number our days, and apply our hearts unto wisdom as we are encouraged to do in Psalm 90:12.

A Time for Everything

We must not waste any more of our precious God-given time that we have left in the earth realm. This should not be a cause for us to be fearful about how much time we may have left upon the earth. It should serve instead as a good reminder that we must be about our Father's business, just like Jesus said He was. Therefore, I encourage you to go through the grieving process as a part of the healing of your broken heart, but please don't grieve too long. Don't allow yourself to get stuck in an "eternal' state of grieving.

God allowed Israel "time" to grieve but it was only for a certain time period. Then they had to move on and continue the journey to fulfill His will for their lives in the earth together. In Deuteronomy 34:8, it says:

"The Israelites grieved for Moses in the plains of Moab thirty days, until the time of weeping and mourning was over."

Going into "overtime" may be good and fun when you are watching different types of sport games, but if you go into overtime in grieving, it could create some very serious long-term problems for you and others connected to you. So, get back in the race and finish your course, because God is not through with you yet. He still has a good plan for your life; that's why you are still here. I know it doesn't feel like it right now, but the best is yet to come! Just know that it won't always be this way. As Carmen use to say all the time, *"this too shall pass!"*

There is a Time to Weep and Mourn

"There is a time for everything, and a season for every activity under the heavens:

a time to be born and a time to die, a time
to plant and a time to uproot, . . . a time to
weep and a time to laugh, a time to mourn
and a time to dance, . . .".

Ecclesiastes 3:1-8 (NIV)

There is a time for everything! Are you prepared
for Him to call "time up" on your weeping and
mourning, and your sorrow and grief? I am confident
that you will be, when the "time" comes!

A Special Note to Caregivers

While I know that *not* everyone's loved ones pass away from some type of sickness prior to death, there are still so many that do. Therefore, I don't want to close out this book without acknowledging the many precious "caregivers" who journey together alongside those who are facing death. Many of you have had to watch your loved ones pass in hospitals, nursing homes, or at their own home. Some even took their last breath in your loving arms. My heart truly breaks for those of you who have went through this type of experience. Most likely, you did everything you knew how to do to preserve their lives for as long as possible.

When my father passed on I experienced what it was like to be a caregiver for the first time. My mother and I had to wash him, and turn him over every two hours, to help keep him from getting bed sores. We fed him until he got to the point where he had to be fed from a feeding tube up until the point of his death. We had to watch him suffering in pain and coughing excessively, to the point where it cracked some of his ribs. It was a very traumatic experience indeed! The next time that I had a similar experience with caregiving, was with Carmen.

Although I was not Carmen's primary caregiver, I did play a role in her care, especially during her hospital stay. I also observed how her family and other family friends rallied together during the entire length of her illness to help. I understand only too well the level of sacrifice family members and other relatives and friends make in serving as caregivers.

Although I was excited about the opportunity to help and serve the woman of God, I also saw how exhausting it can really be, and the pressure it puts on your "soul" and your physical body.

A Measure of Transparency

I was pretty energetic and determined to be a blessing, at the beginning of fulfilling my assignment, as one of those who assisted her. I would go back and forth (by the grace of God) to the hospital every day, pretty much. During this time, Carmen and I had some powerful times in fellowship and personal conversations, as I tended to her as best I could. Many times, Sherisse and I stayed in the hospital with her overnight to give her sister a little break, and also because she was getting to a place where she needed assistance during the night, as well. It was such a blessing for us to be there for her. We were thankful to God that we had been blessed to have the time available to spend with her.

However, by the time Carmen's journey was coming to a close in this expression of life, I began to realize that I was feeling somewhat exhausted. It was all catching up with me—emotionally, physically, and mentally. I even began to get cold symptoms as well. I felt far worse than I was willing to admit at the time. I just didn't want to draw attention to myself, in light of all the suffering my friend and her family were experiencing. I didn't want to admit to anyone how "spent" I was emotionally nor how everything was affecting me, as I was seeking to grasp the reality that her earthly journey was ending very soon.

I wanted to just keep going on and on, until the very end. I wanted to weather the storm no matter the cost! I wanted to do what I felt would be pleasing to God.

I think I had lost my "focus" on drawing strength from my union with God, and had begun to try to make it in my own strength. By that I mean I wasn't "listening" enough to the "wisdom" of God about what I needed to do to get through this in a healthy way.

It was like I had become like a car that is in reality on E, but in denial I just keep on driving, trying in hope to make it to my destination without stopping for gas. Basically, I was still driving on fumes. This is really not wisdom, but in truth we know that most drivers have done that at some time or another! When I was thinking about all of this, I remembered Jesus telling his disciples to,

> **"come aside by yourselves to a deserted place and rest a while. For there were many coming and going, and they did not even have time to eat."**

> **Mark 6:31, 32**

That is just what I needed to do: come aside to a deserted place and rest a while. It wasn't until it was all over that I then realized the full impact that this whole experience had upon my life. I want you to know that I am not sharing this experience with you out of some since of guilt or condemnation, but rather because I have gained some wisdom that I did not have at the time, that I believe can be useful to you now. I am just being honest and transparent about what it is like to care for the sick from a caregiver's perspective. Some of you have been through far worse than I, I am sure.

I just wanted to encourage you in what you have presently been doing for your loved one, or have done for them in the past. It has been done as unto the Lord.

He is the God who sees, and what He sees, He plans to reward! He never forgets the sacrifices we have made for the lives of others (Heb. 6:10). As long as what we are doing is done unto Him, there will be an amazing reward!

The scriptures say in Colossians 3:23-24:

"And whatever you do, do it heartily, as unto the Lord, and not unto men knowing that from the Lord you will receive the reward of the inheritance; for you serve the Lord Christ."

You have not been forgotten! The bible tells us that God honors those who honor him (I Sam. 2:30). You will be rewarded in this life, but more importantly—in the life to come, and that is because God is faithful! He always honors His Word! I hope you will learn much from the experiences that I have chosen to share with you, and the importance of getting wisdom as a caregiver of the sick and shut in.

Now, here are a few timely tips to consider as a caregiver from the past, the present, or the future, just in case you should need to fulfill this "servanthood" position in the years to come.

1. **Cry out for help!** You cannot do it all, as bad as you want to. You would be surprised how many people God will send to "undergird" you in this assignment.
2. **Admit that you are overwhelmed.** *"When my heart is overwhelmed, lead me to the rock that is higher than I."* (Ps. 61:2)
3. **Take a break.** Even if it is only for a few precious moments of the day. Breathe!

4. **Eat!** Even if you don't feel like it. You need to keep your energy and vitality up. Your loved one can sense when you are stressed and near the breaking point!

5. **Get some sleep!** It is your body's opportunity to rejuvenate and refresh itself.

6. **Cry if you need to.** It is a great release of your emotions. Don't always try to be a *tower* of strength for everyone else. We all need support from time to time.

7. **Read your bible.** It is a way of drawing strength from His Word. His words are spirit and they are life! (John 6:63). Read out loud in different translations. Feed your born again spirit off of the Word. It will cheer up your heart and do you good, just like a medicine (Proverbs 17:22).

8. **Don't go on a guilt trip.** Say, *"I'm tired, I feel like I need a break."* God knows and He is the righteous judge.

9. **Share with a trusted friend.** Tell the "truth" about how you are feeling and ask for prayer. You can also do this with your pastor or other clergy too, as led by the Lord. Be sensitive to the Holy Spirit.

10. **Go for a walk or exercise at the gym.** Whatever you do, please move! Your body parts were made to "move". So, stay mobile! It will keep your heart healthy too!

11. **Try to keep up with your regular doctor check-ups.** Especially your blood pressure checks. Too much "stress" can affect your blood pressure.

12. **Please go to church.** Hopefully, you have a spiritual family and a house of worship. There is nothing like being "connected" to a local church home and being in the presence of the Lord together (Heb. 10:25). It is a blessing to be in a loving environment and to be encouraged by your brothers and sisters—in Christ. Everybody needs a good warm hug sometimes too!

13. **Forgive!** Sometimes when people are sick the other family members may not be doing as much as you think they should to help out. This can make you "bitter" and "resentful." Please don't let that get in your heart; just choose to forgive and let it go! Offense will sap your strength. God knows what you are doing through, so cast your care upon Him!

Lastly, if it is now over for you in serving as a caregiver, then you may still need to do some of the same things listed here on a daily basis. Along with the things that apply to you here, I would encourage you to—replenish yourself. You have poured out much, and now you will need a refill.

Why not go out to dinner with friends, take a trip (even a short one will do) or just read a good book! You could also go shopping at the mall, go for a walk with a friend or even go to the gym! Enjoy your God-given life again! After all, He came that you might have and enjoy your life! (John 10:10). Lighten up and laugh a little!

PERSONAL REFLECTIONS FROM
FAMILY AND FRIENDS

Sis. Shartrese Roberson and Min. Joshua Roberson
Family of the Author
Mt. Zion New Covenant Baptist Church
Detroit, MI

Dr. Linda Cobb-McClain (Bio)

A born-again child of God and ordained minister
Graduated from The Bible Training Center at
Word of Faith International Christian Center
Psychotherapist, Ph.D. in Educational Psychology
from University of Michigan, certification

Rev. Doris Moseley and Sis. Sherisse Knight
Sisters in Christ
Mt. Zion New Covenant Baptist Church
Detroit, MI

REFLECTIONS FROM:

Shartrese Roberson

This is going to come as a surprise to some, but when I met Carmen I didn't like her. I guess jealousy was rearing its ugly head, but in my mind it was with good reason. She was a new person seeking to enter in to my mom's circle, and even as a child I was a bit territorial. I call it the only child syndrome. It's the feeling that comes when you feel someone is infringing upon all your time with the one you love. I can still see Carmen and my mom sitting in the car out in front of our house, talking for what seemed like an eternity.

I would stand there and look out the window and flick the porch lights, beckoning my mom to come in the house. Then I would come to the door asking when she was coming in. I couldn't understand what they could possibly be talking about for that long. Now that I'm a bit older, I understand all too well how three hours could pass by when you're talking with a good friend.

Eventually, Carmen grew on me and I started to let her in. I guess I finally realized she wasn't going anywhere. Not only did she grow on me, but I came to love her as if she was a blood relative. I trusted her with my most valuable gift—Joshua (my son)—and developed my own special relationship with her, which has left me with many special memories of my own to cherish. Would you believe I even spent a few hours talking in the car with her myself in front of my house? A full circle moment indeed. That's the beauty of having a true friend. Though she met and befriended my mom first, she understood that my mom and I were a package deal and she loved me just the same.

You see, God knew that I would need an aunt, because all my aunts lived out of state. He knew that I would need someone who understood my mom, who would be there to help me navigate through the rocky moments of our relationship. He knew that I would need a godmother for my son who I could trust if anything happened to me. He knew I would need someone to see about and celebrate my mom when I couldn't.

He knew I would make terrible mistakes, and would need someone grounded in HIS Word to counsel me and pray for me. He knew I would need a boggle partner and a place to go on the holidays for some family fun. He knew I needed someone to take my son to Cedar Point, and someone to give my family rides when we didn't have a car. He knew I would need someone to encourage me to be my best self. Carmen Murray did all that and more.

The bible says, in Psalms 68:6, God puts the single in families. I needed an extended family as I grew into a woman. Life is a journey and we need covenant family to walk with. She walked with each member of my family in her own special way. She helped me to define what it means to be steadfast and unmovable, always abounding in the work of the Lord.

She was an excellent example of what it meant to be a classy lady, confident, godly, and she raised the bar so high that I know I will never meet anyone else like her. In fact, sometimes Carmen was so perfect, I used to tell my mom she wasn't real. I used to say she was an angel. I'm still not convinced she wasn't, but I am convinced she was indeed a friend for the journey. I am forever grateful to have had her in my life, and still blessed by the seeds she sowed in me. I strive each day to continue to make her proud!

REFLECTIONS FROM:

Joshua D. Roberson

The bible says, in the multitude of counselors there is safety (Proverbs 11:14). With the loss of Carmen Murray, part of my safety net was broken. She was my personal intercessor, counselor, and truly my family. I could talk to her about anything. She was always willing to listen and to advise with wisdom. My relationship with her truly preceded her ministry to me. Every year for my birthday Carmen took me out to dinner. Every year for Christmas she would buy socks for me, and I would always laugh and say, *"I bet I know what's in this package,"* and of course I was right every time! She was always making me feel like the favorite.

A little best-kept secret from the past that most people never knew, was that Carmen was my first crush when I was just a little young man. I can recall going to the grocery store and asking my mother for a quarter to get her a ring out of the candy machine. When I got a chance to see her again, I gave it to her. She was so surprised and thrilled to receive it from me. She acted like I had just given her a real diamond ring! She smiled all the way to church that day and showed it off to everyone.

From that time on, Carmen and I did many fun things together. Sometimes it was going on a trip to Cedar Point, and at other times she would invite my family and I over to her house to play card games, to eat, and to have fellowship with her family. Every now and then I even won a few of those games too!

Whatever time you were able to spend with Carmen, you always knew it was going to be fun. It was just fun to be in her presence!

Carmen had a serious side to her though. She was serious about making sure I knew how to pray and lead others to Christ. She was the first person to expose the writer in me, when she asked me to write my thoughts in both of her books. I felt so honored to be asked, considering that I was a rather young man at the time. She valued what I thought and that meant a lot to me.

Auntie Carmen always wanted the best for me and was always excited to see me progress. One time when she was in the hospital I came to see her. My grandmother and Carmen were both looking kind of surprised to see me. They were both trying to figure out how I had got there. My grandmother thought someone had dropped me off. I surprised them both in that I had driven myself in a car I had just purchased on my own, much to their amazement! Carmen was so excited about it. She lifted up her hand (like she would always do), and waved it in the air and put it on her forehead like it was a sign of relief. She knew I had grown into the young man she had invested so much time into.

To say that I miss her is an understatement. I think of her so often and a smile comes to my face. I know that she would be so proud of me and is now cheering me on from the grandstands of heaven, at every growth stage of my life. I also know her impact on my life will be felt in my family for generations to come.

REFLECTIONS FROM:

Dr. Linda Cobb-McClain

FINDING PEACE

And the peace of God which passeth all understanding shall keep your heart and mind through Christ Jesus (Phil 4:7).

I certainly knew Carmen as a "soul sister," over a four-year period, from being connected through an exciting faith-based project that we were both connected to. She struck me as a fervent prayer warrior who always had a heart for the lost. Her ever effervescent smile literally melted your heart when you were in her presence. Talk about a person who exuded peace—she was a diamond in the rough! She exemplified in life the same peace we as children of God are to eventually display, when a loved one dies. However, that's easier said than done, you might say. But we must continue to say it, because it is the Word of God.

As a psychotherapist who has counselled hundreds of children and adults over a 30-year period, I acknowledge and recognize that the grieving process differs in individuals, families, cultures, and is frequently affected by the circumstances which caused one's death. Grief can be especially severe when a loved one's death comes suddenly and before its expected time.

The sudden illness or accident claiming a spouse or child may even trigger a year or more of memory-laden mooning that eventually subsides to a mild depression. For some, the death may seem unbearable.

I recently lost my prayer partner, my spiritual Mom. I lot my biological Mom some years ago, to a botched operation, followed by Dad dying of a broken heart after they had been married for 54 years. I know what it's like to experience that abysmal and empty "hole" where the pit of your stomach cries out over the loss of a loved one, and you think you will never experience the fullness of life again. But I have found the same words, that I've used to comfort others, having had a similar effect on me. I've simply spoken the Word of God, and He healed my heart!

Phil. 4:7

> *His peace will guard your hearts and minds as you live in Christ Jesus (NLT).*
>
> *And God's peace [shall be yours, that tranquil state of a soul assured of its salvation through Christ, and so fearing nothing from God and being content with its earthly lot of whatever sort that is, that peace] which transcends all understanding shall garrison and mount guard over your hearts and minds in Christ Jesus (AMP).*

Mourning and grieving a loved one are normal, shortly following the death of a loved one. However, if you find yourself in that dark place that seems to envelop and overpower your body, soul (mind, will, emotions), and even affecting your spirit so that you feel distance from God, it is the time to draw near to Him.

When you are feeling that emotional pain, pit in your stomach, urge to cry or can't seem to stop crying, or that overpowering feeling of emptiness or just that sense of missing your loved one, just know that—you don't have to stay like that. God has given the Holy Spirit to you as that "relief" valve to give that lift, to get your mind on those things that are just, that are pure, that are praiseworthy! If there be any virtue, that is where He takes you. And when He, "the comforter," who is the Holy Spirit, takes you there and comes upon you in a powerful way, He opens the eyes of your understanding (John 14:26).

There, you will find a peace that even you cannot explain. That peace gets you over the hump, where you find joy in the fact that your loved one is in Heaven and you look forward to one day joining them. That peace gives you strength to see the light at the end of the tunnel and know that the Lord is on your side. He will make a way for you emotionally, psychologically, socially, physically, spiritually and financially. That peace gives you the confidence that your loved one would want you to enjoy life, and not dwell in that dark place of torment and heartache.

Now is the time to be more spiritually productive than ever. It is alright to question God about why your loved one died and, in some instances, He may answer you. It's important to keep those lines of communication open and He is there for comfort, counsel, to give direction and to enfold you under His wings of peace and love. Through the years, several of my questions were answered that addressed why a loved one died, and situations were revealed that I had no knowledge about at the time of my loved one's death.

It's important to remember that we do not grieve as if we have no hope; we have hope because we trust God and we trust in His love. We trust in His goodness and we trust that He is in control of our lives.

Pay attention to the good things God is doing (even in this season, which appears to be a dark place), so that your grief can be mixed with heartfelt gratitude.

Isaiah 41:10

> *Fear thou not; for I [am] with thee: be not dismayed; for I [am] thy God: I will strengthen thee; yea, I will help thee; yea, I will uphold thee with the right hand of my righteousness.*

I've had many former clients come back and testify that their closer walk with God was the most helpful part of the grieving process. Even the professionals in the field of death and dying acknowledge that while bereavement therapy and self-help groups offer support, there is similar healing power in the passing of time, the support of friends, the act of giving support and help to others—especially for those with a strong spiritual foundation.

One of the highlights of Carmen's life is that she left a legacy. She left her footprints on this world through her actions, prayers, praise, jokes, random acts of kindness, the career God placed her in, her ministry, and even her death. Isn't that what life is all about? Carmen was about giving glory to God in life and in her transition.

Recently, at a homegoing I attended, the presiding minister reminded those in attendance of the scripture:

2 Corinthians 5:8

> *We are confident ... to be absent from the body, and to be present with the Lord.*

This text is similar to when they did roll call at school and everyone answered that you were either present or absent. When the class in unison yelled "present," the person was in the room. However, when everyone yelled "absent," it simply meant that they were not at school that day. They may have been at home, skipping class, or out of town; however, we all knew they still existed. Well, in a similar way, Carmen is still around; she simply went to live in her permanent home!

REFLECTIONS FROM:

Rev. Doris Moseley

Proverbs 3:5 says, "Trust in the Lord with all your heart and lean not unto your own understanding." The Message translation says, "Trust God from the bottom of your heart; don't try to figure things out on your own."

Psalms 147:3 says, "He heals the brokenhearted and binds up their wounds." Lastly, in St. John 14:16 Jesus says, "And I will pray to the Father and he will give you another comforter which is the Holy Spirit and He shall abide with you forever."

These three scriptures have meant so much to me in the last several years. Since 2011, I have experienced the death of people who were very close to me and whom I loved dearly. It started with my friend and prayer partner Carmen Murray. To know her was to love and adore her. She was everyone's friend and she made everyone feel special. Whenever I was going through something, Carmen was there to pray with me and encourage me.

Sometimes God would speak to me through her, and she didn't even know that God was using her. Always willing, always loving, always being there for people. She took ill and I knew that if God would heal anybody it would be Carmen, but Carmen went on to be with the Lord.

I really didn't understand why and it kept me perplexed, but I kept hearing the words, *lean not unto your own understanding, His ways are not your ways.*

I won't understand everything; if I did, then he wouldn't be God. And one day God said to me that he loved Carmen more than I ever could. So, that gave me some comfort.

Soon after Carmen passed, my brother passed also. I had two brothers, George and Dennis. Dennis is the baby, and George was the middle child. For over 40 years George was addicted to drugs; they completely controlled his life. About two years before he passed, George got completely delivered from drugs. He was getting his life on track doing a lot of the things he had always wanted to do. I always loved my brother, but our fellowship was limited because of his drug addiction.

Now he was free. We could spend time together and enjoy family gatherings. My children adored George. Two years after his deliverance he became ill, his body shut down quickly and he passed. I was hurt because I thought, why now?

My brothers and I lost our mother in 1987, so I was like a mother and a sister to both my brothers. I walked with my brother George through some of the darkest days of his life. The darkness was now over. He was free to serve God and live the life he always wanted. Why, God?? It was during this time that I began to experience the healing power of God. He healed my broken heart. It was as if a balm was applied to my heart and lifted me out of despair. Healing was slow—but it came.

I experienced the death of my best friend and my children's father, after my brother. These deaths were hard for me also. I wish that I could say that I bounced back right away, but I didn't. But what I did experience was the comfort that the Holy Spirit gives. What an awesome comforter God has given us.

On the outside I was smiling but on the inside I was filled with sadness, uncertainty, and fear. But God!!!

Through my times of fellowshipping with the Holy Spirit I was comforted, I was uplifted, and I was filled with the love of God. The Bible says perfect love casts out fear (I John 4:18). As I determined to build myself up on my most holy faith, praying in the Holy Ghost (according to Jude 20), I received revelation from God that helped me to accept the will of God for the people whose relationship and life was so dear to me. St. John 16:13 says, "When He the Spirit of truth has come; He will guide you into all truth."

But I guess the best of all is, the people who have gone on before us—are not lost. We do not grieve as those who have no hope. This earthly life is not all there is. Our relationships will be restored because they all knew Jesus Christ as their personal Lord and Savior. So, I will see them again; we will be reunited.

So here I am today, healed, full of joy, and determined to continue on in my life and in the things of God. I honor their memory by living, loving, and continuing to be a willing vessel for the Kingdom of God.

Submitted by: Rev. Doris Moseley

REFLECTIONS FROM:

Sherisse Knight

Really, God?

There are some people who God directs to divinely connect into your life so gracefully and effortlessly that you don't recall the true beginning of the relationship's existence. They slip into your inner circle, see through your walls, and tip into your private space. They unselfishly offer a secure listening ear, words of wisdom, faith, prayer, love, and support. They speak life and gentle prophetic declarations over you at significant times. They ignite joy and laughter, and accept you as you are while pushing (often bamboozling) you to be a better you, and to use the gifts that God has placed in you. More importantly, they pierce your heart and remind you what the Word says in every situation. Such was the special relationship with my Friend, my Mentor, my Sister, Carmen Murray. You wonder when did this person become such a cherished and irreplaceable part of your life, but there she was . . .

I admired Carmen's faith, her courage, her sense of humor, even through her own pain, and her constant desire and focus to care for others that she loved, especially her beloved mother, and her dedicated and precious sister Cynthia. I also admired her deep expression of gratitude to those who assisted her in any way. Through words, tokens, grand gestures, and even when she was too weak to motion or speak, there was her illuminating smile or endearing gaze that simply said, "Thank you. I love and appreciate you."

I learned so much from Carmen just by observing her walk in life, and I always knew she was a power house in the spirit. But she was also such a strong, responsible, loving, and compassionate woman in the natural, as well. Her passion and witness for the Lord Jesus Christ were unquestionable and inspiring.

Carmen encountered many people from all walks of life, and she shared herself with everyone. Carmen loved to surprise people, to give gifts great and small, but always full of thoughtfulness and love. It was almost impossible to beat her generosity. However, she was not so great at receiving, and I would often have to argue and even trick her just to treat her to lunch.

Carmen specialized in the intangible and priceless things: love, friendship, faith, hope, strength, and encouragement. Whenever we were able to hang out together, or spend time on the phone, or even in prayer, I always walked away from those encounters feeling like I had been given a gift, like something positive, loving, and edifying had been imparted into me.

We had so many fun, silly times together, serving at church related functions, sharing the dreams for our lives—the hurts, and even the heartbreaks—but little did I know the sobering times that we would also share.

We had planned a wonderful "ladies let our hair down" trip to the Bahamas with a group of friends. Tickets were purchased, and everyone was excited and ready to go. A few weeks before we were to leave, Carmen began to have some back pain. The pain worsened, and she decided to go to the hospital. A few days later, and to the amazement of everyone, Carmen was diagnosed with a late stage of this horrible disease.

I could not believe it when she broke the news to me, and when the doctors came in to speak with her while I was visiting, I attempted to step out of the room to give her some privacy, but she told me not to go. I remember clearly her telling me that this was a public attack (of the devil) and it was going to be a public fight!

I committed to her that day that I would walk this journey with her to her healing, and that we would celebrate her victory together. I had many emotions about this diagnosis, but I quickly realized that I had no time for my emotions. It was just time to love, pray, and fight with Carmen against this disease and the devil.

God had recently blessed me with an opportunity to be able to have freedom in my daily schedule which allowed me a unique opportunity to be available to Carmen and her family, and I took full advantage as God led me in ways that I could help.

Days turned into weeks, and weeks into months, as Carmen's loved ones, the Murray Bible Study Group (a home study which she founded with her Mother and Sister), her entire church family at Mt. Zion New Covenant Baptist Church and many others all over formed a strong group of prayer Warriors to petition God for her healing, to cover her, her family, and the medical staff that would be treating her.

One of many things that impressed me about Carmen, especially during this time, was her acceptance of God's will, her unfailing trust in Him, and her concern for the comfort of others. Carmen knew *who* she was but, more importantly, she knew and embraced *whose* she was, and that made all the difference in her journey throughout this horrible disease.

251

Through it all, Carmen remained a serious threat to the devil. Even while battling this illness, Carmen and her sister Cynthia made a powerful healing CD of scriptures and psalms, and made them available for others to use in their own spiritual warfare. She encouraged herself by listening to this CD constantly as she battled through this illness.

She had tons of visitors and she knew that she was loved. I often felt as if I were back in school, learning about the different treatment options that she chose, sitting in with her on meetings with her doctors and through various surgeries and treatments, documenting her medications, and recording her reactions to the medications as she explained them to me. We discussed scriptures, church, business affairs, and of course looking out for her Mom and Cynthia.

We spent many days and nights together at the hospital. We had "real talk" conversations about God, life, her desires, love, relationships, men, and even death. We talked about fashion, television, future books to be written, and food. She trusted me, and I trusted her. She knew that nothing said between us, or by the doctors, would be too much for me to hear and bear with her, and even through the most challenging of times we would always find something to make us laugh until it hurt.

I felt so helpless at times wanting to take away her pain, and even as the doctors tried to comfort her I knew at some point that they had reached their limits of treatment. But I also knew beyond the shadow of a doubt that our God is limitless.

My faith never wavered that God could heal Carmen.

My fervent prayers were that her healing would take place on this side of Heaven. This disease was tearing away at the tangible physical parts of my sister, but even it had its limits. As I mentioned earlier, Carmen had a gift for specializing in the intangibles!

Carmen's joy was worshipping, sharing the Gospel, and loving on others, and she did that so well. Carmen's life and love were intentional, and that is why I was touched so deeply by her presence and now even still by her physical absence.

Carmen's grasp of her relationship with God made all the difference in her ability to withstand anything, and to lead a life that was pleasing to God.

Through this journey with Carmen I experienced quite a range of different emotions that I could only afford a minuscule of moments in which to allow my flesh to respond. I remember a conversation with my Bishop during which he told me that I didn't have the "luxury "of crying with the family, and he was right. Instead I focused on God's word, but also on understanding directly from Carmen where she was in her heart, assisting in caring for the things that concerned her, and what she wanted at every stage of this journey.

During her illness, and even immediately after her transition, there was no real time for me to deal with my own grief, disbelief, and yet finally acceptance of God's will that Carmen was gone from this earth. It took some time for me to allow grief its "place," and the flood gates that I thought would sometimes be endless did cease.

I grieved for my physical loss of Carmen, and although she had made such an impact and had done so many awesome things in her lifetime, I also found myself grieving for the fact that she didn't get to do some of her heart's desires here on earth that she expressed to me that she really wanted to do. After all, I could not think of anyone who deserved that fulfillment more than she.

I admit that I sometimes questioned God's methods. I had other prayerful close friends who had also been on this journey with Carmen, but there was no one greater that I could turn to assist me with my grief. I knew that no one but God could fully help me with what I was feeling about this whole situation. I also knew that if I stayed plugged into God, he would help me to accept what I did not (or maybe did not want to) understand.

God purposed for me to be on this journey with Carmen and even at the very time of her transition. I knew I was in His will, but I was not happy about His process! But there's something about being in God's will that will somehow give you a peace to endure, to sustain you, and to allow you to do His purpose for placing you in a particular situation. In my life I have sometimes asked the question "Really God?," and His answer is sometimes, "Yes, Really."

Grief involves a certain intentional yielding and it is transitional. I went from wanting what I wanted (that Carmen be healed on this side of Heaven), to the transitions of wanting what she wanted (transitions from earthly healing, to God's will, to being ready to transition), to wanting what God wanted for her (which was to receive her unto Himself).

God brought me through my grieving process, and allows me now to simply rejoice in my memories, lessons learned, laughter and experiences shared, and the ever-present spirit of my dear friend Carmen.

I had past experience enough to know and had already accepted that some things I will not understand here on earth. I had learned early on as a child losing loved ones so close to me that sometimes God says "No," and in Isaiah 55:8, the bible does tell us that His ways are not our ways. Sometimes God really does say "No," but if we remain in the vine and allow Him to minister to us, He is always there willing to navigate us to a **greater** "Yes" in Him.

Sherisse Knight

ACKNOWLEDGEMENTS

CONTINUED

Home Bible Study

To Min. Carmen's Home Bible Study, this book is written to you as well! She loved all of you so very much, and would be rejoicing greatly to know that you are pressing on toward the mark for the prize of the high calling of God in Christ Jesus! She taught you very well! Special thanks to Sis. Mary Eatmon for taking up the teaching mantle as the journey continues.

Family Intercessor

To Rosie and family—mighty intercessor and prayer warrior! I remember when you prophetically spoke that this book was to be. It did not happen quiet like we may have thought it would, but, nevertheless— God did it in His own way and time! He's so faithful!

Called and Ready Writers

To the entire Called & Ready Writers Team: Minister Mary Edwards, the founder of this amazing group, and Sis. Wanda Burnside, the loving president. You have been such an inspiration to both Carmen and I. She loved you all so much! Thanks for the inspiration that kept her moving in her writing career. She and I have both benefited from you all, greatly. Thanks!

Nieces, Nephews, and Godchildren

This book is dedicated also to Carmen's nieces: Cheneia Green, Jasmine Murray, Kiana Murray, and nephew Christan Grant. Carmen's godchildren: Joshua Roberson, Jordan and Jamal Holley, Gabriel Webb, Kristianna Marks, and Jaylen Brown.

Each one of you had a very personal relationship with Carmen, so you know how much she loved you, and the hopes and dreams she had for your future—in Christ. I look forward to seeing some of the fruit of her daily prayers for you all very soon.

Lifetime Friends

To the special one and only sisterhood who were college friends of Carmen's and have remained vitally united with this family over the years: Dr. Linda, Sharon, and Carolyn. This dedication also includes Sis. Sandy, Sis. Pauline, as well as a host of other family and friends far too numerous to mention here. Thanks for all you have done to help our spiritual mother, Shirley Murray, and Cynthia make it through this difficult time in the midst of your own personal pain. Enough can't be said about what you mean to this family. You are a blessing to us all!

Kim Hearns and the Hearns Family

This book is also dedicated to Kim, Carmen's cousin. My heart goes out to you and always will. I know you have been with her all of your life. It's been a tough road to travel for you in light of the close bond you had with her. I pray this little book will be a blessing to help you get through the rest of your Christian journey. Just know that Carmen was so proud of you and the progress you have made in your walk with the Lord! I want to encourage you to stay the course! Also to Kevin, I just want you to know that it was one of the best days of Carmen's life when you accepted Christ as your personal Lord and Savior! We are all excited about your future in Christ!

Last but certainly not least, I have written this book to all those who have been, are now, or will be going through the grieving process, as your loved ones make their departure from this expression of life.

May something that is shared from my heart to yours encourage and strengthen you in some amazing supernatural ways, as you go through the process.

APPENDIX A

THE COVENANT COMMUNITY

A COMMUNITY of God's redeemed people bound together in covenant love, submitted to compassionate authority and rulership and manifesting peace, holiness and family fidelity expressed through revered fatherhood, cherished woman and motherhood with secure and obedient children.

A COMMUNITY where loving correction and instruction produce healthy growth and maturity, where dedication to excellence produces the finest results in arts, crafts, trades and commerce providing prosperity and abundance for all its members.

A COMMUNITY of faith, worship, praise and a selfless ministry manifesting, individually and corporately, the gifts and fruit of the Holy Spirit.

A COMMUNITY where all life is inspired and directed by the Spirit of Jesus Christ and is lived to His glory as a witness and testimony to the world.[24]

—Don Basham

APPENDIX B
THE TERMS OF THE COVENANT
(The One Another Commandments)

Love one another – John 13:34	Admonish one another – Col. 3:16
Build up one another – Rom. 14:19	Comfort one another – I Thess. 4:18
Accept one another – Rom. 15:7	Encourage one another – Heb. 3:13
Care one for another – I Cor. 12:25	Stimulate one another to love and good deeds – Heb. 10:24
Counsel and instruct one another – Rom. 15:14	Confess your sins to one another – Jas. 5:16
Greet one another – Rom. 16:16	Pray for one another – James 5:16
Serve one another – Gal. 5:13	Be hospitable to one another – I Pet.4:9
Forgive one another – Eph. 4:32	Be clothed with humility toward one another– I Pet. 5:5
Be subject to one another – Eph. 5:21	Teach one another – Col. 3:16
Teach one another – Col. 3:16	Lie not to one another – Col. 3:9
Bear one another's burdens – Gal. 6:2	Do not complain against one another – Jas. 5:9
Show forbearance toward one another –Eph. 4:2	Let us not judge one another – Rom. 14:13

APPENDIX C

―――――――∽――――――

WHO I AM IN CHRIST

I AM ACCEPTED IN CHRIST

John 1:12 – I am God's Child.
John 15:15 – I am Christ's friend.
Rom. 5:1 – I have been justified.
I Cor. 6:17 – I am united with the Lord, and I am one with Him in spirit.
I Cor. 6:19-20 – I have been bought with a price. I belong to God.
I Cor. 12:27 – I am a member of Christ's body.
Eph. 1:1 – I am a saint.
Eph. 1:5 – I have been adopted as God's child.
Eph. 2:18 – I have direct access to God through the Holy Spirit.
Col. 1:14 – I have been redeemed and forgiven of all my sins.
Col. 2:10 - I am complete in Christ.

―――――――∽――――――

I AM SECURE IN CHRIST

Rom. 8:1-2 – I am free forever from condemnation.
Rom. 8:28 – I am assured that all things work together for good.
Rom. 8:31-34 – I am free from any condemning charges against me.
Rom. 8:35-39 – I cannot be separated from the love of God.
2 Cor. 1:21-22 – I have been established, anointed, and sealed by God.
Col. 3:3 – I am hidden with Christ in God.

Phil. 1:6 – I am confident that the good work God has begun in me will be perfected.
Phil. 3:20 – I am a citizen of heaven.
2 Tim. 1:7 – I have not been given the spirit of fear, but of power, love, and a sound mind.
Heb. 4:16 – I can find grace and mercy in time of need.
I John 5:18 – I am born of God, and the evil one cannot harm me.

I AM SIGNIFICANT IN CHRIST

Matt. 5:13-14 – I am the salt and light of the earth.
John 15:15 – I am a branch of the True Vine a channel of His life.
John 15:16 – I have been chosen and appointed to bear fruit.
Acts 1:8 – I am a personal witness of Christ's.
I Cor. 3:16 – I am God's temple.
2 Cor. 5:17-21 – I am a minister of reconciliation for God.
2 Cor. 6:1 – I am God's co-worker (I Cor. 3:9).
Eph. 2:6 – I am seated with Christ in the heavenly realm.
Eph. 2:10 – I am God's co-worker.
Eph. 3:12- I may approach God with freedom and confidence.
Phil. 4:13 – I can do all things through Christ who strengthens me.

APPENDIX D

Selection taken from:

NELSON MANDELA
INAUGURAL SPEECH

"Our greatest fear is not that we are inadequate, but that we are powerful beyond measure. It is our light, not our darkness that frightens us. We ask ourselves, "Who am I to be brilliant, gorgeous, handsome, talented and fabulous?" Actually, who are you meant to be? You are a child of God; your playing small does not serve the world. There is nothing enlightened about shrinking so that other people won't feel insecure around you. We were born to make manifest the glory of God within us. It is not just in some; it is in everyone. And as we let our light shine, we consciously give other people permission to do the same. As we are liberated from our fear, our presence automatically liberates others."

APPENDIX E

BOOK RECOMMENDATIONS

1. Bishop Charles L. Middleton Sr., *The Emerging New Breed*, CLM Ministries, 2010.

2. Bishop Charles L. Middleton Sr., *The Life That Pleases God*, CLM Ministries, 2010.

3. Sarah Young, *Jesus Calling*, Thomas Nelson, Nashville, Tennessee, 2004.

4. Mark Vierkler, *4 Keys to Hearing God's Voice*, Destiny Image, 2010.

5. Kay Arthur, *Lord, I Want to Know You*. Waterbrook Press, 2000.

6. Neil T. Anderson, *Who I am in Christ*, Regal Books. Ventura, CA. 2001.

7. Neil T. Anderson. *The Bondage Breaker*. Harvest House Publishers. Eugene, Oregon. 2000.

8. Neil T. Anderson, & Rich Miller. *Walking in Freedom*. Regal Publishing, Ventura, California. 1999.

9. Neil T. Anderson. *Victory Over the Darkness*. Bethany House Publishers. 2000.

10. Joyce Meyer. *Tell Them I Love Them*. FaithWords Publishers. 2003.

11. Joyce Meyer. *Managing Your Emotions.* FaithWords Publishers. 2002.

12. Joyce Meyer. *The Battlefield of the Mind.* Warner Faith. 2002.

13. Kathy Ramsey. *Strength.* Kathy Ramsey Publisher. 2016.

14. Dodie Osteen. *Healed of Cancer.* John Osteen Publisher. 1987.

15. Dr. Betty Price. *Through the Fire.* Faith One Publishers, 2002.

16. A. W. Tozer. *The Knowledge of the Holy.* Harper, San Francisco. 1961.

17. Rick Warren. *The Purpose Driven Life.* Zondervan Publishers. 2013.

18. Sheila M. Bailey. *Makeovers with Leftovers.* Creative Enterprises Studio, Fort Worth, Texas. 2015.

ENDNOTES

[1] Richard J. Foster. *Celebration of Discipline*. Harper & Row, Publishers. New York, N.Y. 1978.
[2]Ibid. p. vi.
[3]Ibid. p. vi.

Chapter 2
[4] Charles L. Middleton Sr. *The Emerging New Breed*. Detroit, MI. Outreach Publishing. 2010. P. 9
[5] Ibid. p. 17
[6] Ibid. p. 17
[7]Ibid. p. 20
[8]Ibid. p. 21

Chapter 3
[9] Charles L. Middleton Sr. *The Life That Pleases God*. Detroit, MI. Charles L. Middleton Ministries. 2011. p. 24

Chapter 7
[10] Charles L. Middleton, Sr. *New Foundations Guide*. Detroit, MI. Outreach Publishing. 1998. p. 24.

Chapter 9
[11] Bogosian, Eric. *Humpty Dumpty*. New York: Dramatists Play Service, 2005. Print.

Chapter 13
[12] Charles L. Middleton Sr. *Preach The Word*. Detroit, MI. Charles L. Middleton Ministries. 2011.

[13] Carmen Murray. *How to Get Your Grove Back*. Detroit, MI. Covenant Outreach Publishing. Detroit, MI. 2001. Print.

Chapter 18

[14] A revision of An *Expository Dictionary of Biblical Words* © 1984 Thomas Nelson, Inc; a compilation of *Nelson's Expository Dictionary of the Old Testament* © 1980 by Thomas Nelson, Inc., and the 1983 fourth printing of An *Expository Dictionary of the New Testament Words* published by Thomas Nelson, Inc.

Chapter 20

[15] Galdone, Paul/G. J. C. *The Three Little Pigs*. Houston Mifflin Harcourt, 2011. Print.

[16] Ibid.

[17] Ibid.

Chapter 21

[18] Carmen D. Murray. *Permission to Grieve*. Detroit, MI. 1997. (Taken from class paper). p. 1

[19] Ibid. p. 1

[20] Ibid. p. 2

[21] Carmen D. Murray. *Victory Over Grief.* Detroit, MI 1997. (Taken from class paper).

Chapter 22

[22] Neil T. Anderson/ Rich Miller. *Walking In Freedom*. Regal Publishing, Ventura, California. 1999. 110

[23] Ibid. p. 111

Appendix A

[24] Don Basham. *The Covenant Community*. (Taken from class notes, 1984), p. 17.

ABOUT THE AUTHOR

Rhonda R. Roberson is an ordained minister serving at Mt. Zion New Covenant Baptist Church of Detroit, under the leadership of Bishop Charles L. Middleton, Sr. and Co-Pastor Mary E. Middleton. Minister Roberson serves as Christian Education Director, and is a member of the Ministerial Alliance and the Intercessory Prayer Team at Mt. Zion. She has a bachelor's degree in Theology from Logos Christian College through the New Covenant Bible Institute of Detroit. Minister Roberson is the dedicated mother of one blessed and highly favored daughter, Shartrese, and one very precious and anointed grandson, Joshua.

To contact Rhonda Roberson for book signings, or speaking engagements:

Email: lohigherground@gmail.com

To purchase copies of her book for individual, book club or group study, go to:
www.Amazon.com

If you enjoyed reading this book, you may also enjoy Rhonda's previous book release, *Let's Stay Together.* It is her passionate push for true love and unity in the body of Christ.

Carmen D. Murray

Sunrise   Sunset
October 6, 1963 — February 12, 2012

"Love Never Fails"

Carmen D. Murray was an ordained minister of Mt. Zion New Covenant Baptist Church in Detroit, under the leadership of Bishop Charles L. Middleton Sr. and Co-Pastor Mary E. Middleton. She was the leader of the Intercessory Prayer Team and a faithful member of our World Christians Outreach Ministry (WCOM), of Mt. Zion. She was a licensed Clinical Social Worker in the State of Michigan. She had a Bachelor of Arts and Master of Social Work from Michigan State University. She received her Masters of Divinity Degree in Theological Studies from the New Covenant Bible Institute in Detroit, Michigan. She was also a faithful member of the "Called and Ready Writer's Guild" of Detroit, MI.

She authored two powerful books: *How to Get Your Groove Back*, which is a practical guide to developing and maintaining an intimate fellowship with God. Also, she wrote *Awaking Love*, which is the diary of a 45 year old virgin. She also created a **healing CD,** where she is quoting various healing scriptures, to encourage the sick. It is set to a beautiful background musical arrangement, create by her sister who is a musician.